探访 中轴

CITY WALKS: BEIJING CENTRAL AXIS EXHIBITION GUIDE

北京京企中轴线保护公益基金会　编著

北京出版集团
北京出版社

图书在版编目（CIP）数据

探访中轴 ：汉英对照 / 北京京企中轴线保护公益基金会编著. — 北京 ：北京出版社，2025.4 — ISBN 978-7-200-19405-0

Ⅰ. TU984.21-49

中国国家版本馆CIP数据核字2025J7P401号

探访中轴
TANFANG ZHONGZHOU

北京京企中轴线保护公益基金会　编著

*

北 京 出 版 集 团
北 京 出 版 社　出版
（北京北三环中路 6 号）

邮政编码：100120

网　　　址：www.bph.com.cn

北 京 出 版 集 团 总 发 行
新 华 书 店 经 销
北 京 华 联 印 刷 有 限 公 司 印刷

*

170 毫米 ×140 毫米　5.8 印张　88 千字
2025 年 4 月第 1 版　2025 年 4 月第 1 次印刷
ISBN 978-7-200-19405-0
定价：56.00 元
如有印装质量问题，由本社负责调换
质量监督电话：010-58572393

编委会

序

中，首先是对时间、空间的一种描述和界定，进而成为中国古代知识体系和价值体系里的一个核心观念和标准。在具体实践中，符合"中"的事物、行为等大多被赋予了尊贵、美好、善良、和合等价值诉求和象征意义。

我国古代都城在选址与规划营建中，将对"中"的追求发挥到了极致，提出"择天下之中而立国，择国之中而立宫"，即在疆域的中心位置定都，在都城的中心位置营建王宫。为进一步强化这种"中"的布局的神圣威严与对称和谐，必须要在"中"之上及周围规划有相应功能与内涵的建筑和空间。这事实上就形成了一条贯通都城核心区域、统领都城空间布局和凸显王权尊贵，并具有对称与韵律之美的都城中轴线。《周礼·考工记》（以下简称《考工记》）将这种理想的都城规划格局概括为"匠人营国，方九里，旁三门。国中九经九纬，经涂九轨，左祖右社，面朝后市，市朝一夫"，涵盖了都城规模、城门布局、道路规划及太庙、社稷坛、宫殿、市廛等的位置、面积等内容。在这样的格局下，中轴线的构成、功能与象征意义无疑得到了最大程度的强调。

在历代都城轴线中，北京中轴线是最接近《考工记》中所描述的理想都城中轴线的范式，堪称中国理想都城秩序的杰作，也是梁思成先生眼中的"世界上就没有第二个"的奇迹。

习近平总书记在北京考察时指出："北京历史文化是中华文明源远流长的伟大见证，要更加精心保护好，凸显北京历史文化的整体价值，强化'首都风范、古都风韵、时代风貌'的城市特色。"而北京中轴线正是积淀厚重的北京历史文化中的杰出范例，是代表这座城市乃至中华文明的"金名片"。要探寻这一皇皇巨制，了解古人的匠心藻思，加入今天的传承保护，不妨从探访中轴线遗产点上的若干古建筑、文物、展览开始。这些展览从相应遗产点在中轴线上的功能和定位出发，诠释相应的历史文化内涵，生动、直观而"接地气"，各美其美、美美与共，构成了以北京中轴线为主题的展览体系，呈现出一幅北京中轴线文化传播的多彩拼图，也是发挥历史博物展览"见证历史、以史鉴今、启迪后人"等功用的绝好例证。

2024年7月27日，在印度新德里举行的联合国教科文组织第46届世界遗产大会通过决议，将"北京中轴线——中国理想都城秩序的杰作"列入《世界遗产名录》，标志着历经十二载，北京中轴线申遗成功，成为中国最具代表性的文化瑰宝之一。

Preface

    "Zhong", initially a description of measurement used in time and space, now has become a core concept and standard in the ancient Chinese knowledge system and value system. In practical terms, things and behavior that conform to "Zhong" are endowed with values and symbolic meanings such as nobility, goodness, kindness, and harmony.

    In the process of siting and planning ancient Chinese capital cities, the pursuit of "Zhong" was taken to the extreme. It was proposed to "choose the center of the world to establish a state, and choose the center of the state to establish a palace." This means selecting the central location within the territory as the capital and constructing the royal palace at the center of the capital. In order to further strengthen the sacredness, symmetry, and harmony of this "Zhong" layout, it was necessary to plan corresponding buildings and spaces based on the concept of "Zhong". This, in fact, gave birth to a central axis that connected the core area of the capital, guided the spatial layout of the capital, and highlighted the dignity of the monarchy with symmetric beauty. *Artificers' Record* summarized this ideal urban planning pattern as follows: "Craftsmen build the capital in the shape of a square with the side length of nine *li*, with three gates on each side. Within the capital, there are nine north-south roads and nine east-west avenues, each of which can accommodate nine carriages running in parallel. To the left is the ancestral temple, and to the right is the altar of land and grain. In front of the palace is the place where courtiers pay homage, and behind it is the market. The market and the place of homage are each a square with sides of one hundred steps." It covers the scale of the capital, the layout of the city gates, road planning, as well as the positions and areas of the imperial ancestral temple, the altar of land and grain, the palace, and the market. In this urban planning pattern, there is no doubt that the construction, function, and symbolic meaning of the central axis are given the utmost emphasis.

Among the axial lines of ancient capitals throughout history, Beijing Central Axis is the closest paradigm to the ideal axial line described in the book *Artificers' Record*. Beijing Central Axis can be regarded as a masterpiece of the ideal urban planning in China and was considered by Liang Sicheng as a unique miracle in the world that has no equal.

President Xi Jinping pointed out during his inspection in Beijing that, "Beijing's rich historical and cultural heritage is a great witness to the long-standing Chinese civilization. We must protect it with greater care, highlight the overall value of Beijing's historical and cultural heritage, and strengthen the city's characteristics as the capital, an ancient city and a city which reflects the spirit of the times." The Beijing Central Axis is an outstanding example of the profound historical and cultural heritage of Beijing. It is a "golden business card", representing not only the city itself but also the Chinese civilization as a whole. To explore this grand project, understand the ingenuity of ancient craftsmen, and contribute to its preservation in modern times, one can start by going to the historic buildings, cultural relics, and exhibitions at various heritage sites along the central axis. These exhibitions are based on the functions and positioning of corresponding heritage sites along the central axis, interpreting their historical and cultural connotations in a vivid, intuitive, and down-to-earth manner. Each of these exhibitions presents the beauty of their respective subjects while sharing a common beauty, forming an exhibition system centered around Beijing Central Axis. They present a colorful mosaic of cultural dissemination along the central axis and serve as excellent examples of historical museum exhibitions that fulfill functions such as witnessing history, drawing lessons from the past, and enlightening future generations.

On July 27, 2024, the UNESCO World Heritage Committee, at its 46th session held in New Delhi, India, adopted a decision to inscribe "Beijing Central Axis: A Building Ensemble Exhibiting the Ideal Order of the Chinese Capital" on the *World Heritage List*. This marks the successful inscription of Beijing Central Axis after twelve years of dedicated nomination efforts, establishing it as one of China's most representative cultural treasures.

目　录
CONTENTS

北京中轴线展讯
Beijing Central Axis Exhibition Guide

探访北京中轴线
Exploring Beijing Central Axis

永定门　Yongdingmen Gate

中轴线南段道路遗存　Southern Section Road Archeological Sites

先农坛　Altar of the God of Agriculture

天坛　Temple Of Heaven

正阳门　Zhengyangmen Gate

天安门广场及建筑群　Tian'anmen Square Complex

外金水桥　Outer Jinshui Bridges

天安门　Tian'anmen Gate

端门　Upright Gate

社稷坛　Altar of Land and Grain

太庙　Imperial Ancestral Temple

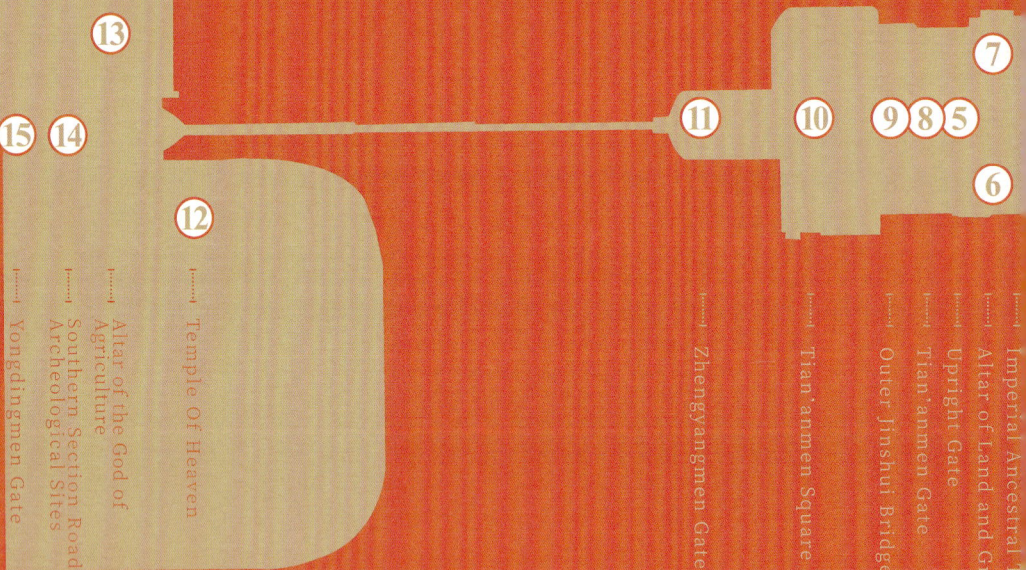

13　15　14　12　11　10　9　8　5　7　6

景山

万宁桥

钟鼓楼

③

②

①

Jingshan Hill

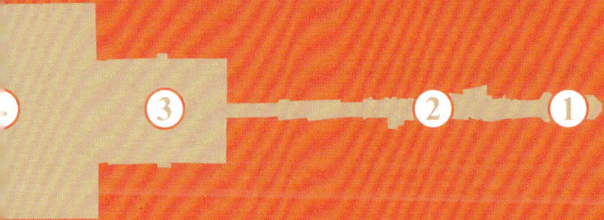

Wanning Bridge

Bell and Drum Towers

南——北

　　北京中轴线位于北京老城中心，纵贯老城南北，全长 7.8 公里，始建于 13 世纪，形成于 16 世纪，此后不断完善，历经逾 7 个世纪，是统领整个老城规划格局的建筑与遗址的组合体。北京中轴线北端为钟鼓楼，向南经万宁桥、景山，过故宫、端门、天安门、外金水桥、天安门广场及建筑群、正阳门、中轴线南段道路遗存，至南端永定门，太庙和社稷坛、天坛和先农坛分列中轴线东西两侧。这些遗产构成要素涵盖了古代皇家宫苑建筑、古代皇家祭祀建筑、古代城市管理设施、国家礼仪和公共建筑、居中道路遗存 5 种不同类型的历史遗存，联系起宏伟、庄严的国家礼仪场所和繁华、热闹的市井街市，并形成了前后起伏、左右均衡对称的景观韵律与壮美秩序，是中国传统都城中轴线发展至成熟阶段的典范之作。

Beijing Central Axis runs north-south through the heart of the old city of Beijing, totaling 7.8 kilometers in length. It was initially constructed in the 13th century and shaped in the 16th century. With continuous refinement over seven centuries, Beijing Central Axis is an ensemble of building complexes and archeological sites, which governs the overall layout of the old city. At the northern end of the Axis are the Bell and Drum Towers; it then runs south through the Wanning Bridge, the Jingshan Hill, the Forbidden City, the Upright Gate, the Tian'anmen Gate, the Outer Jinshui Bridges, the Tian'anmen Square Complex, the Zhengyangmen Gate, and the Southern Section Road Archeological Sites, to the Yongdingmen Gate at the southern terminus of the Axis. The Imperial Ancestral Temple, the Altar of Land and Grain, the Temple of Heaven, and the Altar of the God of Agriculture are located on the east and west sides of the Axis. The components can be organized into five types comprising imperial palaces and gardens, imperial sacrificial buildings, ancient city management facilities, national ceremonial and public buildings, and central axis road remains. The layout connects the state ceremonial sites with the city facilities, forming a rhythmic cityscape that creates a well-balanced, symmetrical, and magnificent sense of order. It is an outstanding example of the central axis of traditional Chinese capital cities at a mature stage of development.

钟鼓楼

钟鼓楼

钟鼓楼坐落于北京中轴线北端，高耸于北京传统街区之中。鼓楼、钟楼南北纵置，两座建筑之间由一个长方形广场连接。明清时期，钟鼓楼承担着城市计时与报时的功能，为重要的城市管理设施，见证了中国古代钟、鼓报时的传统生活方式。钟鼓楼建筑气势恢宏，以高大的体量成为老城内城中的制高点，是俯瞰中轴线北段的重要视点。

Bell and Drum Towers

The Bell and Drum Towers are located at the north end of Beijing Central Axis, standing tall in the traditional neighborhoods of Beijing. The Bell Tower and Drum Tower are vertically aligned from north to south, connected by a rectangular square. The towers were significant city management facilities for time keeping and announcing, bearing witness to the traditional way of life. The architectural grandeur of Bell and Drum Towers is magnificent. With their large volume and height, they are the most imposing structures in the old city's inner city area with commanding views over the northern section of Beijing Central Axis.

钟楼
Bell Tower

鼓楼
Drum Tower

02

万宁桥

万宁桥

　　万宁桥位于地安门外大街中部、什刹海东岸，南北跨越于玉河水道之上。桥体为单拱石桥，由桥体、雁翅、镇水兽、澄清上闸遗存构成。万宁桥始建于元代，是北京中轴线上最为古老的桥梁，其位置及功能历经 7 个多世纪始终未变，为元大都、明清与当代北京城中轴线的叠压关系提供了重要的物质实证。

Wanning Bridge

  The Wanning Bridge is located in the middle of Di'anmen Outer Street on the east bank of Shichahai Lake and spanning the Yuhe River. The Wanning Bridge is a single-arch stone bridge. It comprises the bridge, *yanchi* slabs, the Water-harnessing Beasts, and the Chengqing Upper Watergate Remains. The Wanning Bridge is the oldest bridge on Beijing Central Axis. Its location and function have remained unchanged for over seven centuries. The structure contains layered information from various periods of history and provides vital material evidence of the superimposed relationship of Beijing Central Axis from the Yuan Dynasty to modern China.

万宁桥
Wanning Bridge

万宁桥
Wanning Bridge

万宁桥局部
Partial view of Wanning Bridge

镇水兽
The Water-harnessing Beast

03

景 山

Jingshan Hill

景山

　　景山坐落于北京中轴线上，为明清两代皇家御苑。其与故宫共同组成的布局关系，展现了中国宫苑的传统规划理念。景山平面呈形态规整的长方形，可分为南北两个区域。南部以景山山体为主，山脊上以中轴线对称建有五亭，北部区域居中建有寿皇殿建筑群。景山以其独特的园林景观和人造山体，兼具礼仪祭祀和登高游赏眺望全城的双重功能，为明清时期的国家礼仪传统提供了实物见证，成为北京中轴线上的制高点与重要景观节点。

Jingshan Hill

The Jingshan Hill towers over Beijing Central Axis. It was the imperial garden of the Ming and Qing dynasties. Its position and relationship to the north of the Forbidden City demonstrate the planning concept of Chinese palaces and gardens. The general layout of the Jingshan Hill presents itself as a regular rectangle. It is divided into northern and southern parts. Dominating the southern part is the artificial hill, with five pavilions lying symmetrically with the Axis on the hill ridge. In the northern part stands the building complex of the Hall of Imperial Longevity, aligned on the Axis. With its unique garden landscape, the Jingshan Hill has dual functions for both sacrificial rituals and the artificially created mountain setting providing a high elevation from which to look out over the city. It testifies to the imperial ceremonial and ritual traditions carried out in the Qing Dynasty, and is the tallest point as well as a key skyline node on Beijing Central Axis.

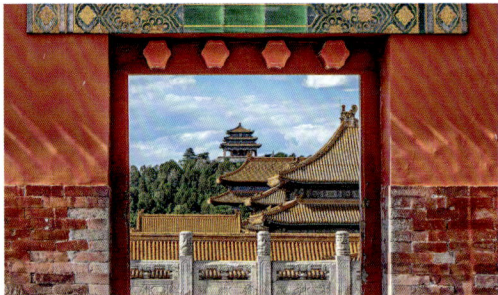

景山
Jingshan Hill

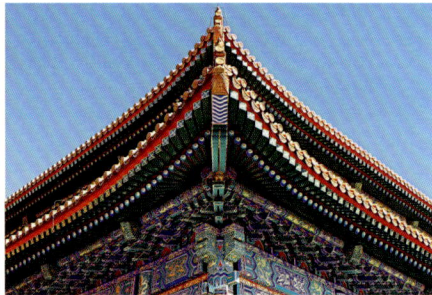

景山建筑一角
Partial view of the building complex at Jingshan Hill

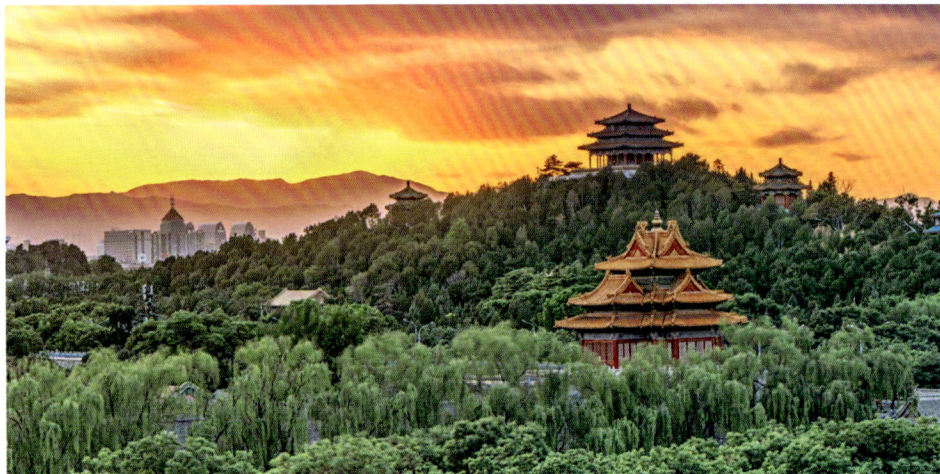

万春亭
The Wanchun Pavilion (Eternal Spring Pavilion)

04

故宫

Forbidden City

故宫

　　故宫为明清两代的宫城，是中国皇家宫殿建筑的杰出典范，其规划格局反映出"象天法地""择中立宫"的中国都城规划理念。故宫以中路为中轴线，南北可分为外朝区和内廷区两大区域。故宫是明清时期皇家举办国家庆典、处理政务和生活起居的场所，见证了中华文明多元一体格局的发展。故宫博物院的成立成为北京中轴线公众化进程的重要节点。

Forbidden City

The Forbidden City was the palace city of the Ming and Qing dynasties, and is an outstanding example of Chinese royal palace architecture. Its location and layout epitomize the ancient Chinese concept of urban planning of "building the imperial palace at the central location" and "modeling heaven and earth." The Forbidden City consists of building complexes, with the middle section on the axis. It also comprises an Outer Court area and an Inner Court area from the south to the north. The Forbidden City was a place where the imperial families hosted national celebrations, administered government affairs, and enjoyed daily activities. It has witnessed the Chinese cultural tradition of inclusion and diversity. The establishment of the Palace Museum marks an important step in the development of Beijing Central Axis toward public access.

故宫一角
A corner of the Forbidden City

故宫角楼
Corner Tower at the Forbidden City

午门
The Meridian Gate

A panoramic view of the Forbidden City

05

端门

Upright Gate

端门

端门位于故宫以南，天安门以北，是明清两代进出宫城的前导性礼仪建筑序列的组成部分，为朝堂空间的一部分。端门由城台和城楼组成，建筑形制和体量与天安门城楼基本相同，两者以其高大的形体和端庄的风姿，烘托出皇城与皇宫轴线建筑的威严和神圣。

Upright Gate

The Upright Gate stands south of the Forbidden City and north of the Tian'anmen Gate. The Upright Gate was an essential part of the leading space for ritual activities before entering and exiting the palace city and part of the imperial court. Comprising the terrace and the gate tower, it is similar to the Tian'anmen Gate in its design and size. Together with the Tian'anmen Gate, the Upright Gate features a towering volume and a solemn style, highlighting dignity and divinity of central axis buildings in the palace city and the imperial city.

端门南立面
The south facade of the Upright Gate

06

太庙

Imperial Ancestral Temple

太庙

　　太庙位于故宫东南侧，与社稷坛以北京中轴线东西对称布局，体现了《考工记》所载"左祖右社"的理想都城规划范式。太庙建筑群坐北朝南，由内垣墙和外垣墙围合成两重环套式长方形院落。主要祭祀建筑均位于内垣，居中对称分布。太庙作为明清两代皇家祖庙，是中国祖先崇拜文化传统的物质载体，是重要的国家礼制建筑，也是中国现存最完整、规模最大的皇家祖先祭祀建筑群。今天，太庙作为北京市劳动人民文化宫对外开放。

Imperial Ancestral Temple

The Imperial Ancestral Temple is located southeast of the Forbidden City and faces the Altar of Land and Grain, both of which are symmetrically arranged on the west and east sides of central axis. It embodies the ideal capital city's planning paradigm as prescribed in the *Artificers' Record*. According to this paradigm, the ancestral temple must be built on the left, while the altar of land and grain must be on the right. The building complex faces south and comprises a rectangular courtyard with inner and outer courtyard sections. Most sacrificial buildings are located in the inner courtyard section, symmetrically laid out along the axis. Serving the imperial families of the Ming and Qing dynasties, the Imperial Ancestral Temple is the material carrier of the Chinese cultural tradition of "worshiping the ancestors". It is an essential building for national rituals and the most complete and largest extant building complex of ancestral worship by the imperial families. Today, the Imperial Ancestral Temple is open to the public as the Beijing Working People's Cultural Palace.

太庙享殿
The Sacrificial Hall of the Imperial Ancestral Temple

太庙建筑局部
Partial view of the Imperial Ancestral Temple

享殿牌匾
Plaque of the Sacrificial Hall

太庙建筑局部
Partial view of the Imperial Ancestral Temple

享殿排水口雕刻螭首
The carving of Chishous at the drainage outlets of the Sacrificial Hall

07

社稷坛

Altar of Land and Grain

社稷坛

　　社稷坛位于故宫西南侧，与太庙以北京中轴线对称布局，体现了《考工记》所载"左祖右社"的理想都城规划范式。建筑群由内外两重坛墙围合成环套式院落，中央设祭坛。社稷坛是中国现存最为完整的古代皇家祭祀太社和太稷的祭坛，反映出中国传统文化中对国土的认识和崇拜，以及祈求国家政权与疆土永固的愿望。社稷坛作为北京第一处转变为城市公园的皇家建筑，呈现了北京中轴线公众化的转变历程。

Altar of Land and Grain

The Altar of Land and Grain is located southwest of the Forbidden City, opposite the Imperial Ancestral Temple symmetrically on both sides of the central axis, which embodies the ideal capital city's planning paradigm as prescribed in the *Artificers' Record*. The building complex comprises a ring-style courtyard with inner and outer courtyard sections. The altar stands in the center. The Altar of Land and Grain is the most complete ancient imperial altar in China that was used to worship Tai She and Tai Ji. It reflects the comprehension and worship of land and the desire for the eternity of the country and territorial integrity in traditional Chinese culture. As the first imperial building turned into an urban park in Beijing, the Altar of Land and Grain also reflects the transformation to the increased public accessibility of Beijing Central Axis.

社稷坛
The Altar of Land and Grain

08

天安门

天安门

　　天安门位于北京中轴线上，在端门以南，外金水桥以北，面朝天安门广场。天安门以城楼为主体建筑，城楼北侧设一对华表，城楼南侧设石狮两对、华表一对，均以北京中轴线东西对称布局。天安门是明清时期颁布诏令及现代举行重大国事活动的场所，是国家礼仪的载体，见证了 2000余年王朝统治的终结与中华人民共和国的成立。1949 年 10 月 1 日，中华人民共和国开国大典在天安门举行，标志着中华人民共和国的诞生。

Tian'anmen Gate

 The Tian'anmen Gate sits on Beijing Central Axis, south of the Upright Gate and north of the Outer Jinshui Bridges, facing Tian'anmen Square. The gate tower is the main structure of the gate, with a pair of ceremonial columns known in Chinese as *huabiao* on its north side. There is another pair of *huabiao*, joined by two pairs of stone lions, on the south side, all standing and sitting west-east of the central axis symmetrically. The Tian'anmen Gate was where the emperors of the Ming and Qing dynasties issued their imperial edicts. It remains as a venue for major national celebrations. The founding ceremony of the People's Republic of China (PRC) was held here on October 1st, 1949, proclaiming the birth of the PRC.

《康熙南巡图》
Kangxi Emperor's Southern Inspection Tour

中华人民共和国万岁

世界人民大团结万岁

天安门
Tian'anmen Gate

天安门
Tian'anmen Gate

09

外金水桥

外金水桥

　　外金水桥位于天安门南侧，纵跨于东西向的外金水河上，共有7座桥体，以北京中轴线为中心对称布局。居中5座桥体分别与天安门城楼的5个券门相对；东西两侧各一座桥体分别与太庙、社稷坛的南门相对。作为进入明清皇城的先导区域，外金水桥是明清两代由皇城通向南郊祭祀的必经之路，也是如今国家举办重大庆典活动的礼仪空间，始终承担着重要的礼仪功能。

Outer Jinshui Bridges

The Outer Jinshui Bridges are located on the south side of the Tian'anmen Gate and span the Outer Jinshui River meandering west to east. There are seven bridges symmetrically distributed along the central axis, five of which face the five arched gateways through the terrace of the Tian'anmen Gate. The other two bridges face the south gates of the Imperial Ancestral Temple and the Altar of Land and Grain respectively. They have borne an important ceremonial function since their inception. In the Ming and Qing dynasties, it was used for entering and exiting the imperial city, and served as passage from the Forbidden City to the southern suburbs when the emperor went out to participate in worship ceremonies. Today, it is still an essential part of the ceremonial space where important state celebrations are hosted.

外金水桥
Outer Jinshui Bridges

10

天安门广场及建筑群

天安门广场及建筑群

　　天安门广场及建筑群位于北京中轴线的核心位置，已成为国家重大活动、人民文化活动和大型庆典活动的举办地，自形成至今始终是国家礼仪文化传承的见证。天安门广场及建筑群由天安门广场、人民英雄纪念碑、毛主席纪念堂、人民大会堂、中国国家博物馆共同构成，其规划格局延续并强调了以北京中轴线均衡对称的原则，其建筑与景观展现出中国20世纪中叶公共建筑对民族风格的探索与创新，是中国城市规划和建筑发展的里程碑。

Tian'anmen Square Complex

Tian'anmen Square Complex is located at the heart of Beijing Central Axis. It is the preeminent venue for hosting state-level activities and cultural events as well as grand celebrations for the people. Ever since its inception, the square complex has witnessed the historical continuity of China's state ritual traditions. Tian'anmen Square Complex consists of Tian'anmen Square, the Monument to the People's Heroes, the Chairman Mao Memorial Hall, the Great Hall of the People, and the National Museum of China. The square's planning respects and emphasizes the principle of the Axis' balance and symmetry. The architecture and landscape of the Tian'anmen Square Complex demonstrate China's efforts in modern times to explore and innovate on the national style in the design of public buildings in the mid-20th century. These interventions reflect important milestones in the progress of urban planning and architectural design in the modern era.

人民大会堂
The Great Hall of the People

中国国家博物馆
The National Museum of China

毛主席纪念堂
The Chairman Mao Memorial Hall

人民英雄纪念碑
The Monument to the People's Heroes

11

正阳门

Zhengyangmen Gate

正阳门

正阳门位于天安门广场南端，由纵置的城楼与箭楼两座高大建筑构成，城楼居北，箭楼居南。作为明清时期北京内城正南门，正阳门是北京内、外城中规模最大、形制等级最高的城门建筑，见证了中国传统城市管理方式，是登高眺望天安门广场及建筑群和北京中轴线南段景观的重要景观视点。

Zhengyangmen Gate

Located at the southern end of Tian'anmen Square, the Zhengyangmen Gate comprises two tall buildings oriented north-south, with the gate tower in the north and the archery tower in the south. As the central south gate of the inner city of Beijing in the Ming and Qing dynasties, the Zhengyangmen Gate is the largest and highest-ranked city gate among the gates of inner and outer cities, and has witnessed the traditional way of urban management in ancient China. It is one of the key viewpoints to enjoy a distant view of the Tian'anmen Square Complex and an important part of the landscape in the southern section of Beijing Central Axis.

正阳门箭楼
The Archery Tower of the Zhengyangmen Gate

正阳门城楼
The Gate Tower of the Zhengyangmen Gate

12

天坛

Temple of Heaven

天坛

　　天坛位于北京老城外城东南部，北京中轴线东侧，与先农坛以北京中轴线为中线东西对称布局，突显出中国传统都城规划对礼仪的尊重与强调。天坛是中国现存规模最大、保存最为完整的明清皇家祭天建筑群，由内坛和外坛两部分组成，两重坛墙呈北圆南方。内坛以东西隔墙为界，分为南北两个坛域。南部坛域以圜丘坛建筑群为核心，北部坛域以祈谷坛建筑群为核心，两者通过丹陛桥构成的南北主轴线连接。天坛是中国古代皇家祭祀建筑的杰作，承载着明清两代国家祭天礼仪与文化传统。

天坛
Temple of Heaven

Temple of Heaven

The Temple of Heaven sits in the southeast of the outer city of the old city of Beijing, symmetrically facing the Altar of the God of Agriculture on the other side of the central axis. It highlights the respect and emphasis on rituals and order in Chinese capital city planning. The Temple of Heaven is China's largest and best-preserved Ming and Qing-era building complex for heaven-worshiping ceremonies. It comprises the inner and outer sections, surrounded by walls which are round in the north and square in the south. The south area of the inner section centers around the Altar of Circular Mound Complex, and the north area centers around the Altar of Prayer for Grain Complex, with the Red Stairway Bridge connecting these two areas and forming a north-south axis in the Temple of Heaven. The Temple of Heaven is a masterpiece of ancient Chinese royal sacrificial architecture. It is a carrier of national heaven-worshiping rituals and cultural traditions of the Ming and Qing dynasties.

皇穹宇
The Imperial Vault of Heaven

天坛祈年殿
The Hall of Prayer for Good Harvests at
the Temple of Heaven

祈年殿藻井
The caisson ceiling of the Hall of Prayer
for Good Harvests

从圜丘坛望皇穹宇
The view of the Imperial Vault of Heaven
from the Altar of Circular Mound

天坛
Temple of Heaven

天坛祈年殿
The Hall of Prayer for Good
Harvests at the Temple of Heaven

13

先农坛

Altar of the God of Agriculture

先农坛

先农坛位于北京老城外城西南部，与天坛以北京中轴线为中线东西对称布局。先农坛由内坛与外坛组成，内坛核心祭祀建筑群包括先农坛、耤田、观耕台与太岁殿建筑群，附属建筑包括神仓建筑群、神厨建筑群与具服殿。外坛建有神祇坛和庆成宫等。先农坛作为中国现存古代规模最大的皇家祭祀农神之所，展现出中国传统社会对农耕文化的尊重，承载着明清两代皇家祭祀先农的礼仪传统。

Altar of the God of Agriculture

The Altar of the God of Agriculture is located southwest of the outer city of the old city of Beijing, symmetrically facing the Temple of Heaven on the other side of the central axis. The area of the Altar of the God of Agriculture consists of the inner and outer sections. Ritual buildings in the inner section comprise the Altar of the God of Agriculture, the Ceremonial Farmland, the Plowing Viewing Platform, the Hall of the God of the Year Complex. etc. In the outer section are the historical courtyards of the Altars of Spirits of Heaven and Earth and the Qingcheng Palace Complex. As the largest existing ancient Chinese venue for imperial sacrificial ceremonies in honor of the God of Agriculture, the altar reveals how traditional Chinese society showed respect for its agrarian culture. It is thus a carrier of the ceremonial traditions of the Ming and Qing dynasties that offered sacrifices to the God of Agriculture.

太岁殿
The Hall of the God of the Year

祭坛
The Altar

庆成宫
The Qingcheng Palace

14

中轴线南段道路遗存

中轴线南段道路遗存

  中轴线南段道路遗存为若干处分布于正阳门至永定门的居中道路遗存。截至 2022 年年底，南段道路遗存由自北向南分布的珠市口南中轴道路排水沟渠遗址、永定门内中轴历史道路遗存、永定门北侧石板道遗存构成。北京中轴线南段居中道路是古代皇帝从宫城至南郊祭祀的必经之路。这些遗存以物质实证真实地展现出自明代以来南段居中道路的位置、走向、工程构造和不断传承沿用的历史，见证了北京中轴线延续至今的国家礼仪文化。

Southern Section Road Archeological Sites

The Southern Section Road Archeological Sites comprise a series of central road remains from the Zhengyangmen Gate to the Yongdingmen Gate, including the Drainage Ditch Site, South of Zhushikou, the Road Foundation Site, North of the Yongdingmen Gate, and the Stone Road Site, North of the Yongdingmen Gate from south to north. The southern section road was on the route that had to be passed for national rituals and ceremonies during the Ming and Qing dynasties. The Southern Section Road Archeological Sites are the material evidence that irrefutably show the location, orientation, engineering techniques, and history of continuous use of the central road, and bear witness to the state ritual traditions that have continued on Beijing Central Axis to this day.

中轴线南段道路遗存
Southern Section Road
Archeological Sites

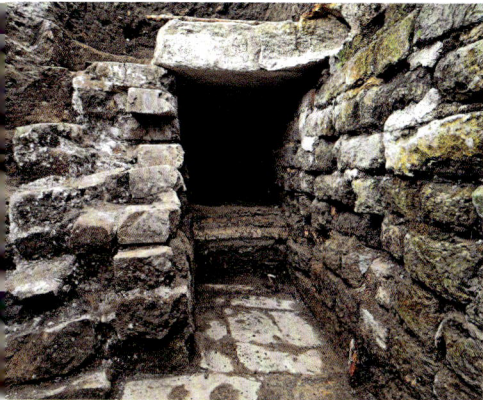
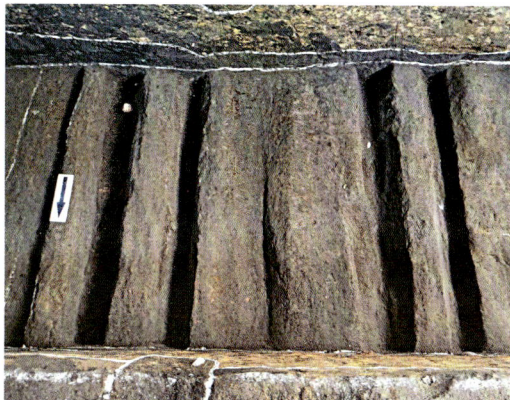

中轴线南段道路遗存
Southern Section Road Archeological Sites

15

永定门

永定门

永定门坐落于北京中轴线南端，为北京老城外城正南门，见证了明清城市传统管理方式。现存永定门为 2005 年严格遵循中国文物保护原则完成重建的地标性建筑，由重建的城楼建筑及南侧瓮城地面标识构成。永定门以城楼的建筑形象标识出北京中轴线南端的位置，展示出中国古代城楼建筑传统形式与工艺做法，成为眺望北京中轴线南段景观的重要视点。

Yongdingmen Gate

The Yongdingmen Gate is located at the southern end of Beijing Central Axis. As the south gate of the outer city of the old city of Beijing, it provides a unique testimony to the methods of traditional urban management during the Ming and Qing dynasties. The existing Yongdingmen Gate is a historical landmark for marking the site of the original gate which was rebuilt in 2005 following the Principles for the Conservation of Heritage Sites in China. It comprises the reconstructed gate tower and the pavements on the ground showing the historic placement of the wengcheng (a defensive endosure) on the south side. The location of the gate tower marks the position of Beijing Central Axis' southern end, exhibiting the traditional forms and architectural techniques applied in constructing gate towers in ancient China. It is an essential scenic spot for viewing the landscape of the southern section of Beijing Central Axis.

永定门
Yongdingmen Gate

从永定门城楼北眺
中轴线南段
North view of the Beijing
Central Axis from the
Yongdingmen Gate Tower

009

永定门
Yongdingmen Gate

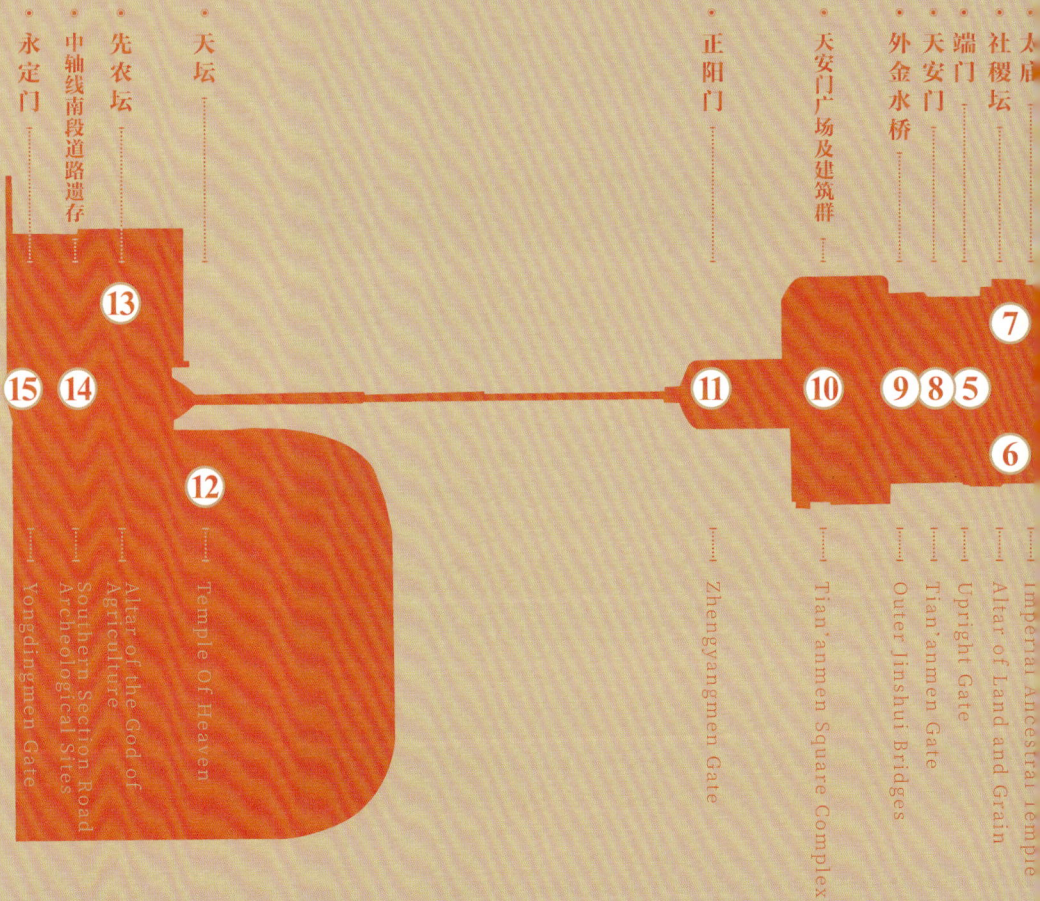

永定门
Yongdingmen Gate

中轴线南段道路遗存
Southern Section Road Archeological Sites

先农坛
Altar of the God of Agriculture

天坛
Temple Of Heaven

正阳门
Zhengyangmen Gate

天安门广场及建筑群
Tian'anmen Square Complex

外金水桥
Outer Jinshui Bridges

天安门
Tian'anmen Gate

端门
Upright Gate

社稷坛
Altar of Land and Grain

太庙
Imperial Ancestral Temple

⑮ ⑭ ⑬ ⑫ ⑪ ⑩ ⑨ ⑧ ⑤ ⑦ ⑥

· 景山

· 万宁桥

· 钟鼓楼

③

②

①

Jingshan Hill

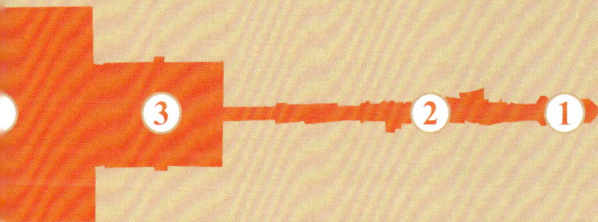

Wanning Bridge

Bell and Drum Towers

南——北

北京中轴线已建立多种形式的公众宣传教育体系，通过研究出版、多媒体运用、网络平台、专题研讨会、主题宣传教育活动、传统文化传承与体验活动等，全方位、多渠道地宣传北京中轴线的遗产价值、历史发展、遗产保护理念等内容，提升公众的文化遗产保护传承意识。

举办博物馆展览活动是实现社会教育功能的重要方式。相关遗产点正通过在北京中轴线上的适当场所，举办系统的、不断更新的展览，将文化遗产的历史、普遍价值与保护理念等推介给观众，以提高社会参与度，这也是遗产生命力的源泉所在。固本培元，方得长久。

The public promotion and education system of Beijing Central Axis has been established, incorporating various means of promotion, including research publications, multimedia applications, online platforms, thematic seminars, thematic promotional activities, traditional cultural inheritance and experiential events, etc. Through comprehensive and multi-channel means, it aims to promote heritage value, historical development, and heritage conservation concepts of Beijing Central Axis. The goal is to enhance public awareness of cultural heritage preservation and inheritance.

Museum exhibitions are an important means of social education. In suitable venues along Beijing Central Axis, through systematic and continuously updated exhibitions, the history, universal value, and conservation concepts of cultural heritage are introduced to the visitors, with the aim to stimulate and enhance social participation. This is also where the vitality of heritage lies. By establishing a solid foundation and nurturing the essence, long-term sustainability can be achieved.

钟鼓楼

鼓楼展览包括二层"中国古代计时仪器展"固定陈列和一层"时间的故事"常设展览。

中国古代计时仪器展

鼓楼二层"中国古代计时仪器展"是原状陈列展，展品包括 25 面报时更鼓、铜刻漏、碑漏、时辰香、日晷等中国古代计时仪器复制品。计时仪器是时间文化的重要组成部分，也是人类社会走向文明的重要标志。自 2001 年起，北京市钟鼓楼文物保管所深入挖掘历史文化，先后复制了 25 面报时更鼓及计时仪器碑漏、铜刻漏、时辰香和日晷，完整展现了中国古代的 4 种计时仪器。"中国古代计时仪器展"可以带你了解中国古代计时仪器的计时原理，弘扬中华民族传统司时文化。鼓楼二层每日定时有击鼓表演，观众既可以欣赏击鼓表演，也可以在鼓楼二层南外廊远眺北京中轴线风景。

展览地点：鼓楼二层
展览时间：长期
主办单位：北京市钟鼓楼文物保管所

Bell and Drum Towers

The Drum Tower exhibition includes a permanent display on the 2nd floor called "Exhibition of Timekeeping Devices in Ancient China" and a permanent exhibition on the 1st floor called "The Story of Time."

Exhibition of Timekeeping Devices in Ancient China

The "Exhibition of Timekeeping Devices in Ancient China" on the 2nd floor of the Drum Tower is an *in situ* display. The exhibits include reproductions of 25 striking drums, bronze clepsydras, stele-shaped timekeepers, incense clocks, and sundials, which are ancient Chinese timekeepers. Timekeeping instruments are important components of time culture and significant symbols of human society's progress toward civilization. Since 2001, the Beijing Bell and Drum Towers Cultural Relics Preservation Institute has delved deeply into historical culture and replicated 25 striking drums and timekeeping instruments such as the stele-shaped timekeepers, bronze clepsydras, incense clocks, and sundials, presenting a complete display of the four types of ancient Chinese timekeepers. The "Exhibition of Timekeeping Devices in Ancient China" will help you understand the working principles of ancient Chinese timekeeping instruments and promote the traditional Chinese culture of timekeeping. On the 2nd floor of the Drum Tower, there are regular drum performances at specific times each day. Visitors can enjoy a drum performance or have a panoramic view of the central axis from the south outer corridor of the Drum Tower.

Exhibition Location: the 2nd floor of the Drum Tower

Exhibition Duration: Permanent

Organizer: Beijing Administrative Office for Cultural Heritage of the Bell and Drum Towers

柜香漏
Closet incense holder

漏香柜

中国古代计时仪器展
Exhibition of Timekeeping Devices
in Ancient China

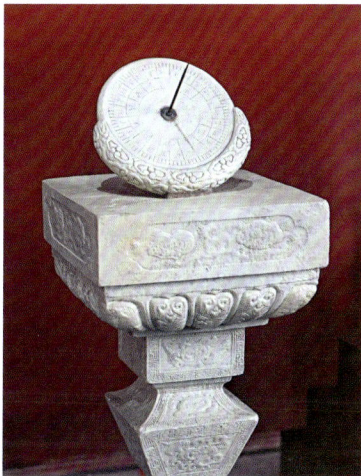

"时间的故事"钟鼓楼历史文化展

　　"时间的故事"钟鼓楼历史文化展共展出 10 件藏品、48 件辅助展品和装置、6 部数字影片及 12 个交互体验展项。观众可以循着钟鼓之声在充满仪式感的 720° 全景沉浸式空间内自由漫步，体验四重数字光影艺术下鼓楼的时空变幻，了解钟鼓楼的建筑历史和特色、计时报时运行机制，回溯它和北京中轴线的时光流逝及保护传承故事，感受历史与我们的温暖共生。

展览地点：鼓楼一层
展览时间：长期
主办单位：北京市钟鼓楼文物保管所

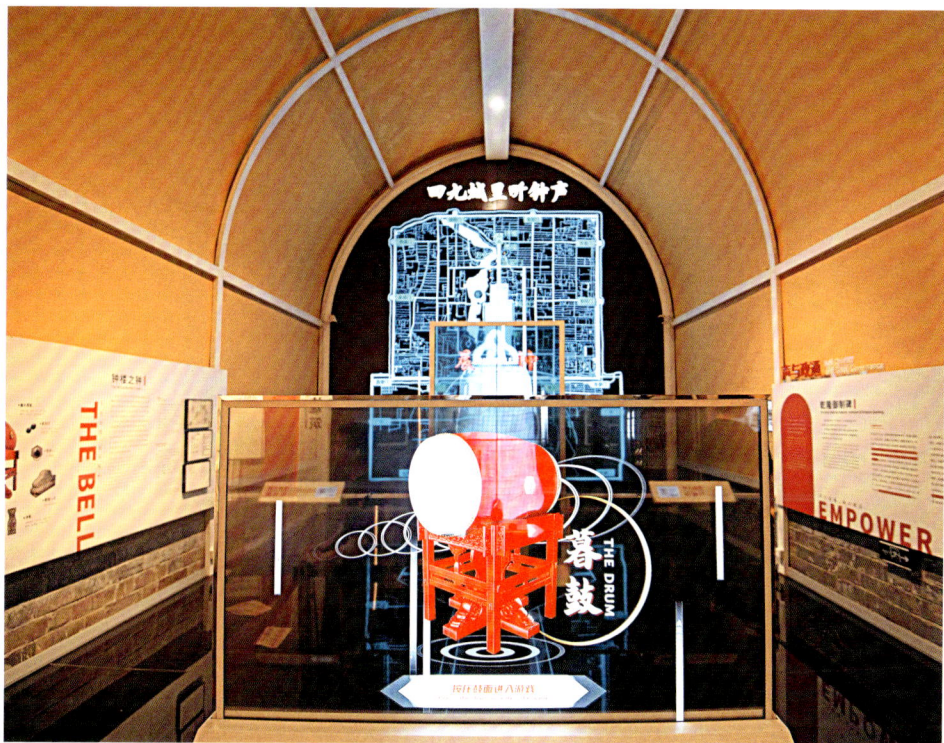

"The Story of Time" Bell and Drum Towers Historical and Cultural Exhibition

The exhibition "The Story of Time" showcases 10 items, 48 auxiliary exhibits and installations, 6 digital films, and 12 programs offering interactive experiences. Visitors can freely explore the immersive 720-degree space filled with ceremonial ambiance, guided by the sound of bells and drums. They can experience the changes of the Drum Tower in the past through four-dimensional digital light and shadow art, and gain an understanding of the architectural history and features of the Drum Tower and the operating mechanisms of timekeepers. They can also take a journey back in time, exploring the stories of the passing years between the Tower and Beijing Central Axis and the preservation of heritage, feeling the touch of history.

Exhibition Location: the 1st floor of the Drum Tower

Exhibition Duration: Permanent

Organizer: Beijing Bell and Drum Towers Cultural Relics Management Office

景山

景山寿皇殿历史文化展

　　寿皇殿展览以正殿局部原状展陈和其他配殿主题展览相结合的方式展示景山寿皇殿建筑群的历史文化。其中，寿皇殿中轴线上的戟门和寿皇殿为局部原状陈列展，以实物复原形式进行展示。依据可资参考的历史照片、故宫文物仿制复原龛位、供案、器具，寿皇殿正殿内仿制了 74 件家具，遵循"重视依据、有法可循"的原则，再现皇家祭祀的历史情境，展示中华传统祀礼文化。东配殿、西配殿和神厨通过实物展示、图文展板、文献复制、实体沙盘及多媒体演示等展示手段，分别从祀礼、建筑、历史 3 个维度，以学术的态度，展览的语言，"述而不论、引经据典"的原则，诠释儒家仁孝文化，弘扬中华民族优秀传统文化。

展览地点：寿皇殿建筑群
展览时间：长期
主办单位：北京市景山公园管理处
官方网站：景山公园
　　　　　http://www.bjjspark.com

Jingshan Hill

Hall of Imperial Longevity Historical and Cultural Exhibition

The exhibition showcases the historical and cultural significance of the Hall of Imperial Longevity Complex of Jingshan Hill through a combination of the part of the main hall's *in situ* display and thematic exhibitions in the side halls. The Halberd Gate, and the Hall of Imperial Longevity itself are displayed in their original state. Based on physical restorations that were derived from historical photographs and collections in the Forbidden City, niches, offering tables, and utensils were replicated. In the Hall of Imperial Longevity, 74 pieces of furniture have been reproduced to recreate the historical atmosphere of royal rituals, exhibiting traditional Chinese sacrificial culture following the principle of "relying on evidence and following established practices." The east and west side halls and the divine kitchen employ various exhibition methods such as physical displays, graphic panels, document replicas, architectural scale models, and multimedia presentations. Through these means, they interpret Confucian culture of benevolence and filial piety, and promote excellent traditional Chinese culture from three dimensions: sacrificial rituals, architecture, and history, with an academic approach and exhibition language based on the principle of "describing without comments, citing classics and references."

Exhibition Location: The Hall of Imperial Longevity Complex

Exhibition Duration: Permanent

Organizer: Municipal Administrative Office of the Jingshan Park, Beijing

Official Website: Jingshan Park
http://www.bjjspark.com

景山寿皇殿历史文化展
Hall of Imperial Longevity Historical and Cultural Exhibition

景山寿皇殿历史文化展
Hall of Imperial Longevity Historical and Cultural Exhibition

故宫

故宫的展览包括原状陈列展、专题展、临时展览等。

原状陈列展

原状陈列展是故宫博物院历史悠久、极具特色，且深受广大观众喜爱的展览类型。在故宫内的主要大殿，如太和殿、保和殿、中和殿、乾清宫、交泰殿、坤宁宫等，宫殿中的陈设都是严格遵循历史档案记载选择与布置的，力求恢复历史原貌，让观众能够真切地感受到浓厚的历史文化氛围。这些历尽沧桑的古代建筑与精美的文物藏品一起构成和谐统一的整体，蕴含着丰富的历史信息和文化内涵，向世人形象地展示了宫廷文化。

展览地点：故宫博物院
展览时间：长期
主办单位：故宫博物院
官方网站：故宫博物院
https://www.dpm.org.cn/Home.html

Forbidden City

The exhibitions at the Forbidden City include reconstructed interior display exhibitions, thematic exhibitions, and temporary exhibitions.

Reconstructed Interior Display Exhibitions

The reconstructed interior display exhibition is a type of exhibition in the Palace Museum that has a long history with unique characteristics, and is loved by a wide range of visitors. In the main halls of the Forbidden City, such as the Hall of Supreme Harmony, Hall of Preserving Harmony, Hall of Central Harmony, Palace of Heavenly Purity, Hall of Union, and Palace of Earthly Tranquility, the furnishings are selected and arranged strictly according to historical records, aiming to restore the historical appearance and allow visitors to experience the profound historical and cultural atmosphere. These ancient and weathered buildings, together with the exquisite cultural collections, form a harmonious and unified whole, containing rich historical information and cultural connotations, vividly showcasing the court culture to the world.

Exhibition Location: The Palace Museum

Exhibition Duration: Permanent

Organizer: The Palace Museum

Official Website: Palace Museum
https://www.dpm.org.cn/Home.html

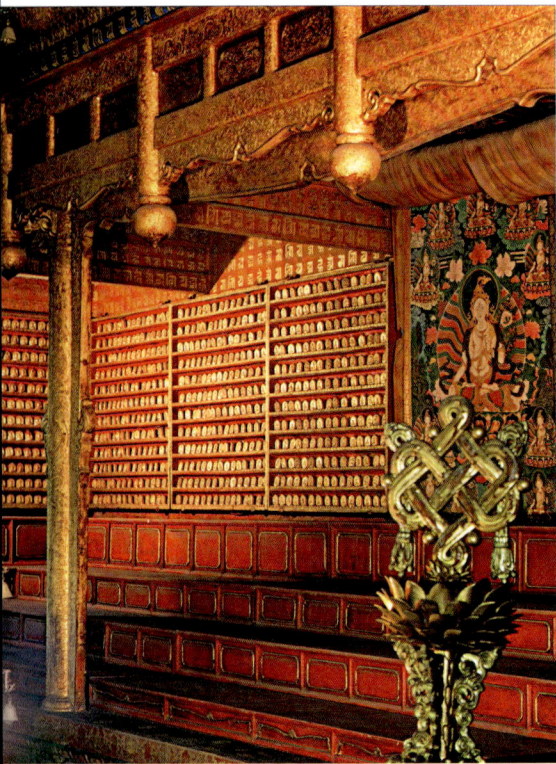

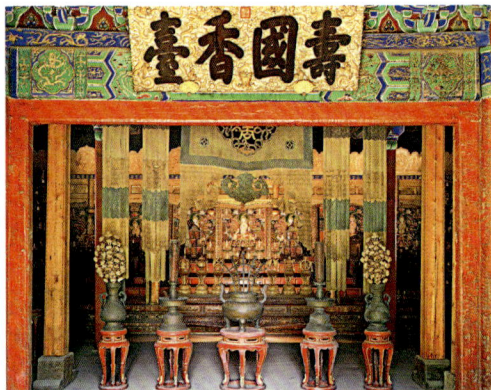

原状陈列展
Reconstructed Interior Display Exhibitions

专题展

　　故宫博物院目前藏有 180 余万件（套）文物，其中绝大多数属于清宫旧藏。这些藏品中有的源自历代皇室的递次收藏，有的是宫廷营造机构奉旨造办，另外也有各地的进贡礼品。这些文物历经岁月淘洗，成为中华民族悠久历史和灿烂文化的物证。为展示这些珍贵文物，故宫开设专题展馆，主要有珍宝馆、钟表馆、家具馆、雕塑馆等。观众置身于传统宫殿景观中，可以细细品味这些奇珍异宝的旷世之美。

展览地点：故宫博物院
展览时间：长期
主办单位：故宫博物院
官方网站：故宫博物院
　　　　　https://www.dpm.org.cn/Home.html

Thematic Exhibitions

The Palace Museum currently houses 1.8 million cultural relics, the vast majority of which belong to the former imperial collection of the Qing Dynasty. These collections include items that were collected by successive imperial families and created by court institutions under imperial orders, as well as tribute gifts from various regions. These artifacts have withstood the test of time and serve as physical evidence of the long history and splendid culture of the Chinese nation. In order to showcase these precious cultural relics, the Palace Museum has established special exhibition halls, including the Treasure Gallery, Clock and Watch Gallery, Furniture Gallery, and Sculpture Gallery. Visitors can immerse themselves in the traditional halls and appreciate the unparalleled beauty of these rare treasures.

Exhibition Location: The Palace Museum

Exhibition Duration: Permanent

Organizer: The Palace Museum

Official Website: Palace Museum
https://www.dpm.org.cn/Home.html

太庙

大庙中轴——太庙历史文化专题展

　　"大庙中轴——太庙历史文化专题展"分为5个章节。第一章"太庙概述"，介绍太庙服务于中国古代的宗庙制度，位于中轴之左，与社稷坛以中轴线为中线东西对称布局，体现出"左祖右社"的理想都城格局；第二章"太庙历史"，通过永乐始建、弘治增建、嘉靖改制、清代沿用、太庙新生5个阶段的内容，介绍北京太庙自建成至今的历史；第三章"太庙祭祀"，从祭祀仪式和祭祀流程两个方面，辅以场景复原和视频影像，展现太庙的祭祀文化；第四章"太庙建筑"，展示太庙独具一格的建筑构造，并展示享殿模型；第五章"祭器祭品"，展示太庙祭祀所用的祭器祭品。展览在严谨的学术论证和资料考察的基础上，以相关领域专家研究成果为基础，从多个角度介绍了太庙之于北京中轴线的文化内涵。

展览地点：太庙（北京市劳动人民文化宫）
展览时间：长期
主办单位：北京市总工会
承办单位：北京市劳动人民文化宫
官方网站：北京市劳动人民文化宫（太庙）
　　　　　http://www.bjwhg.com.cn

大庙中轴——太庙历史文化专题展
The Grand Temple on the Central Axis—History and Culture of the
Imperial Ancestral Temple Thematic Exhibition

Imperial Ancestral Temple

> **The Grand Temple on the Central Axis—History and Culture of the Imperial Ancestral Temple Thematic Exhibition**

The exhibition is divided into five parts. Part 1 provides an overview of the Imperial Ancestral Temple, introducing its role in the ancient Chinese ancestral temple system. Located on the left side of the central axis, it follows a symmetrical layout with the Altar of Land and Grain on the west side of the central axis, embodying the ideal capital layout of "ancestral temple on the left, while the altar of land and grain on the right." Part 2 focuses on the history of the Temple, covering five stages: construction during the Yongle Emperor's reign, reconstruction during the Hongzhi Emperor's reign, restructuring during the Jiajing Emperor's reign, continued use during the Qing Dynasty, and revitalization in modern times. It highlights the historical development of the Imperial Ancestral Temple in Beijing. Part 3 explores the sacrificial rituals of the Temple, showcasing the sacrificial culture of the Temple with the focus on sacrificial ceremonies and procedures, through scene reconstructions, and video footage. Part 4 showcases the distinctive architectural structure of the Temple, including a model of the Sacrificial Hall. Part 5 presents the sacrificial objects and offerings used in the ceremonies held at the Temple. It provides insights into the ceremonial items used and their symbolic meanings. The exhibition is based on rigorous academic research and extensive data analysis, drawing on the research achievements of experts in relevant fields. It offers a multi-dimensional exploration of the cultural significance of the Imperial Ancestral Temple to the Beijing Central Axis.

大庙中轴——大庙历史文化专题展

The Grand Temple on the Central Axis—History and Culture of the
Imperial Ancestral Temple Thematic Exhibition

Exhibition Location: The Imperial Ancestral Temple (Beijing Working People's Cultural Palace)

Exhibition Duration: Permanent

Sponsor: Beijing Federation of Trade Unions

Organizer: Beijing Working People's Cultural Palace

Official Website: Beijing Working People's Cultural Palace (Imperial Ancestral Temple)
http://www.bjwhg.com.cn

大庙中轴——太庙历史文化专题展
The Grand Temple on the Central Axis—History and Culture
of the Imperial Ancestral Temple Thematic Exhibition

131

社稷坛

中山公园园史展

　　展览分为"宫禁右掖　皇家祭坛""源远流长　国之大典""辟治公园　首开风气""与时俱进　传承发展"4个章节，首次以大量珍贵史料和园藏文物，辅以科技化展示手段，系统展示社稷坛建成604年以来、中山公园开放110周年以来的发展变迁。

展览地点：中山公园
展览时间：长期
主办单位：中山公园
官方网站：中山公园（社稷坛）
　　　　　http://www.zhongshan-park.cn

Altar of Land and Grain

Exhibition on the History of Zhongshan Park

The exhibition is divided into four sections: "The Imperial Altars and Forbidden Grounds," "A Longstanding Tradition of National Rites," "From Imperial Grounds to Public Park," and "Progress and Inheritance through Time." For the first time, it presents a systematic display of the 604-year-old history of the Altar of Land and Grain and the 110-year-old evolution of Zhongshan Park since its public opening, through a large collection of rare historical literature and artifacts, enhanced by technological display methods.

Exhibition Location: Zhongshan Park

Exhibition Duration: Permanent

Organizer: Zhongshan Park

Official Website: Zhongshan Park (Altar of Land and Grain)

http: www.zhongshan-park.cn

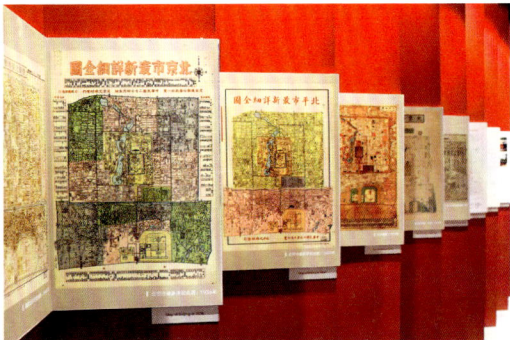

中山公园园史展
Exhibition on the History of Zhongshan Park

中山公园园史展
Exhibition on the History of Zhongshan Park

中国国家博物馆

中国国家博物馆的展览包括基本陈列、专题展览和临时展览等。

古代中国陈列

"古代中国陈列"是中国国家博物馆的基本陈列之一，它以王朝更替为主要脉络，分为远古时期、夏商西周时期、春秋战国时期、秦汉时期、三国两晋南北朝时期、隋唐五代时期、辽宋夏金元时期和明清时期 8 个部分。该陈列以古代珍贵文物为主要载体，较为全面地展示了古代中国不同历史时期在政治、经济、文化、社会生活及中外交流等方面的发展状况，突出展现了中华文明绵延不绝的发展特点和各族人民共同缔造多民族国家的历史进程，展现了中华民族取得的辉煌成就和对人类文明做出的伟大贡献。

展览地点：中国国家博物馆地下一层展厅
展览时间：长期
主办单位：中国国家博物馆
官方网站：中国国家博物馆
　　　　　http://www.chnmuseum.cn

National Museum of China

The exhibitions at the National Museum of China include the basic display, thematic exhibitions, and temporary exhibitions.

Ancient China Exhibition

"Ancient China Exhibition" is one of the basic exhibitions at the National Museum of China. It is organized around the dynastic changes and divided into eight sections: prehistoric times, Xia, Shang, and Western Zhou dynasties, Spring and Autumn and Warring States Periods, Qin and Han dynasties, Three Kingdoms, Jin and Southern and Northern dynasties, Sui, Tang, and the Five dynasties, Liao, Song, Xixia, Jin and Yuan dynasties, and Ming and Qing dynasties. This exhibition primarily showcases ancient precious cultural relics, comprehensively presenting the development of ancient China in terms of politics, economy, culture, social life, and international exchanges during different historical periods. It highlights the continuous development of Chinese civilization and the historical process of multiple ethnic groups jointly creating a multi-ethnic nation. It also demonstrates the splendid achievements of the Chinese nation and its great contributions to human civilization.

Exhibition Location: Exhibition Hall on the Basement 1st floor of the National Museum of China

Exhibition Duration: Permanent

Organizer: The National Museum of China

Official Website: National Museum of China
http://www.chnmuseum.cn

古代中国陈列
Ancient China Exhibition

141

专题展览

　　中国国家博物馆拥有藏品 140 余万件（套），涵盖了从远古时期到当代各个历史阶段社会发展变化的不同方面。中国国家博物馆注重发掘展品本身的内在价值，发挥其在展览中的印证历史、具象化历史的独特作用。中国国家博物馆立足馆藏，策划长期专题展览，如"科技的力量""中国古代钱币展""中国古代玉器艺术""中国古代瓷器展"等。

展览地点：中国国家博物馆各专题厅
展览时间：长期
主办单位：中国国家博物馆
官方网站：中国国家博物馆
　　　　　http://www.chnmuseum.cn

Thematic Exhibitions

The National Museum of China houses a collection of over 1.4 million items, covering various aspects of social development from prehistoric times to the contemporary period. The museum emphasizes the intrinsic value of the exhibited items and showcases their unique role in providing evidence and tangible historical context. Based on its collection, the National Museum of China plans long-term thematic exhibitions such as "The Power of Technology," "Exhibition of Ancient Chinese Coins," "Art of Ancient Chinese Jade," "Exhibition of Ancient Chinese Porcelain," and so on.

Exhibition Location: Thematic exhibition halls at the National Museum of China

Exhibition Duration: Permanent

Organizer: The National Museum of China

Official Website: National Museum of China
http://www.chnmuseum.cn

正阳门

"北京中轴线——中国理想都城秩序的杰作"专题展览

北京中轴线位于北京老城中心，纵贯老城南北，由 15 处遗产要素构成，是统领整个老城规划格局的建筑与遗址的组合体。它由古代皇家宫苑建筑、古代皇家祭祀建筑、古代城市管理设施、国家礼仪和公共建筑、居中道路遗存组成，自 13 世纪始建，至 16 世纪成型，此后不断完善，历经 7 个多世纪，形成了秩序井然、气势恢宏的城市建筑群，见证了影响中国都城营建传统 2000 余年的理想都城秩序，是中国都城中轴线的典范之作。

展览从北京中轴线的遗产描述、列入理由、保护与管理 3 个层面详细阐述，呈现了所有承载北京中轴线作为世界遗产突出普遍价值的构成要素，以及对北京中轴线所施行的整体保护与管理，并突出中轴线作为一个整体的城市空间序列所具有的真实性与完整性。

展览地点：正阳门箭楼
展览时间：长期
主办单位：北京市文物局　北京中轴线申遗保护工作办公室
资助单位：由北京京企中轴线保护公益基金会和腾讯公司共同设立的"中轴基金"资助

Zhengyangmen Gate

> ### Thematic Exhibition "Beijing Central Axis: A Building Ensemble Exhibiting the Ideal Order of the Chinese Capital"

The Beijing Central Axis is in the heart of the old city of Beijing, running through the north and south of the city. It consists of 15 heritage sites and is a combination of buildings and ruins that dominate the entire layout of the old city. It is composed of ancient royal palace and garden architecture, ancient royal sacrificial buildings, ancient urban management facilities, national ritual and public buildings, as well as the remnants of central roads. It was established in the 13th century and took shape in the 16th century. Since then, it has been continuously improved and developed over more than 7 centuries, forming an orderly and magnificent urban architectural complex. It bears witness to over 2,000 years of traditional capital construction in the Chinese capital and represents the ideal central axis in a capital city.

Based on this, the Beijing Central Axis embarked on the journey of World Heritage nomination. The exhibition provides a detailed description of the heritage value, reasons for nomination, and protection and management of the Beijing Central Axis. It presents all the constituent elements that highlight the outstanding universal value of the Axis as a World Heritage site, as well as the comprehensive protection and management measures implemented for the Axis. It emphasizes the authenticity and integrity of the Beijing Central Axis as an essential part of urban planning.

Exhibition Location: The archery tower of the Zhengyangmen Gate

Exhibition Duration: Permanent

Organizer: Beijing Municipal Cultural Heritage Bureau, Beijing Central Axis Nomination and Conservation Office

Sponsor: Zhongteng Foundation, jointly established by the Beijing Central Axis Conservation Foundation and Tencent Holdings Limited

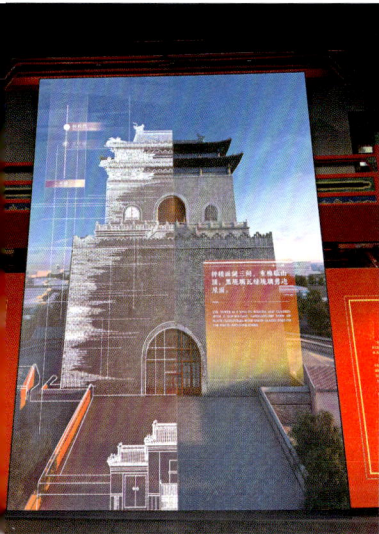

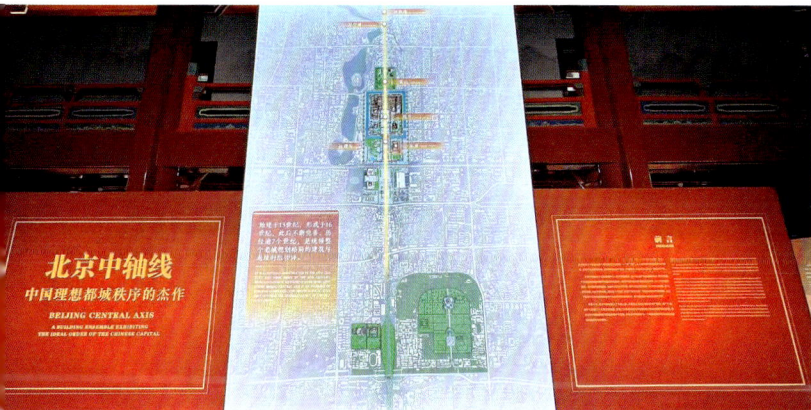

"北京中轴线
——中国理想都
城秩序的杰作"
专题展览
Thematic Exhibition
"Beijing Central Axis:
A Building Ensemble
Exhibiting the Ideal
Order of the Chinese
Capital"

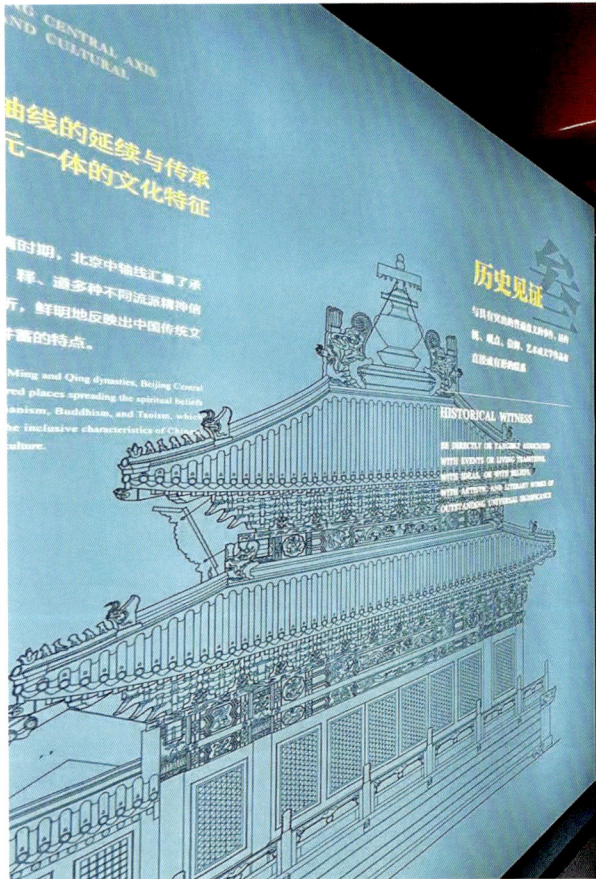

轴线的延续与传承
元一体的文化特征

...西时期，北京中轴线汇聚了承
...释、道多种不同流派精神信
...所，鲜明地反映出中国传统文
...并蓄的特点。

...Ming and Qing dynasties, Beijing Central
...ed places spreading the spiritual beliefs
...anism, Buddhism, and Taoism, whi...
...he inclusive characteristics of Chin...
...culture.

历史见证

与其有关的当代最文...特征、...
体、观点、信息、艺术或文学作品...
直接或有形的联系

HISTORICAL WITNESS

BE DIRECTLY OR TANGIBLY ASSOCIATED
WITH EVENTS OR LIVING TRADITIONS
WITH IDEAS, OR WITH BELIEFS
WITH ARTISTIC AND LITERARY WORKS OF
OUTSTANDING UNIVERSAL SIGNIFICANCE

"北京中轴线
——中国理想都
城秩序的杰作"
专题展览,
Thematic Exhibition
"Beijing Central Axis:
A Building Ensemble
Exhibiting the Ideal
Order of the Chinese
Capital"

149

天坛

走进斋宫——天坛斋宫历史文化展

　　"走进斋宫——天坛斋宫历史文化展"包括"天坛：北京中轴线的明珠""斋宫：静心自省的圣域""循礼：明清祭天斋戒"3 个专题和明清两代历史原状陈设展示，同时增加了演示北京中轴线斋戒御制诗和楹联匾额等内容。该展全面介绍了中国传统祭祀斋戒文化，及其蕴含的敬畏天道、恭谦自警的理念，以及追求人与自然和谐统一的精神，对现代人回归自然、重拾身心自律，颇具借鉴价值。

展览地点：天坛斋宫无梁殿
展览时间：长期
主办单位：北京市天坛公园管理处
官方网站：天坛公园
　　　　　http://www.tiantanpark.com

走进斋宫——天坛斋宫历史文化展
Get Closer to the Fasting Palace – History and Culture about the Fasting Palace Exhibition

Temple of Heaven

**Get Closer to the Fasting Palace—
History and Culture about the Fasting Palace Exhibition**

The exhibition includes three thematics: "The Temple of Heaven: A Shining Pearl inlaid in the Capital City," "The Fasting Palace: A Holy Place for Meditation and Seif-alert," "Following Ceremonial Rituals: Fasting before Worshiping the Heaven during Ming and Qing periods," as well as historical permanent exhibitions of Ming and Qing dynasties. At the same time, it also includes demonstrations of imperial poetry and couplets and plaques for fasting on Beijing Central Axis. This exhibition comprehensively introduces the traditional Chinese sacrificial fasting culture, which embodies the spirit of reverence for the Heaven, humility and self-caution, as well as the pursuit of harmonious unity between humans and nature. It has great reference value for modern people to return to nature and regain physical and mental self-discipline.

Exhibition Location: Beamless Hall of the Fating Palace at the Temple of Heaven
Exhibition Duration: Permanent
Organizer: Municipal Administrative Office of the Temple of Heaven, Beijing
Official Website: Temple of Heaven Park
                 http://m.tiantanpark.com

皇帝亩洒水瓶（仿铜）

走进斋宫——天坛斋宫历史文化展
Get Closer to the Fasting Palace—History and Culture about the Fasting Palace Exhibition

走进斋宫——天坛斋宫历史文化展
Get Closer to the Fasting Palace—History and Culture about the Fasting Palace Exhibition

走进斋宫——天坛斋宫历史文化展
Get Closer to the Fasting Palace—History and Culture about the Fasting Palace Exhibition

先农坛

庆成宫原状陈设

2024 年 12 月 21 日，有着 560 多年历史的北京先农坛庆成宫首次面向社会公众开放。庆成宫原名斋宫，建于明天顺二年（1458 年），是明清两代帝王在祭祀先农前斋戒的场所。清乾隆二十年（1755 年），对其连廊与墙体进行改建，形成现有格局，并更名为庆成宫，成为皇帝祭享先农、亲耕耤田礼成后的庆贺之所。据史料记载，文武百官在此向皇帝表示礼成庆贺，而后皇帝为百官赐茶，由顺天府率大兴、宛平县令至庆成宫东掖门报耤田终亩数，礼成后皇帝乘舆离开。

展览地点：北京先农坛庆成宫
展览时间：长期
主办单位：北京市文物局
官方网站：先农坛（北京古代建筑博物馆）
　　　　　http://www.bjgjg.com
资助单位：北京京企中轴线保护公益基金会

Altar of the God of Agriculture

Reconstructed Interior Display of Qingcheng Palace

On December 21, 2024, Qingcheng Palace at the Altar of the God of Agriculture in Beijing, boasting a history of over 560 years, was opened to the public for the first time. Originally named the Palace of Abstinence, it was built in 1458 (the 2nd year of the Tianshun era of the Ming Dynasty) as the place where emperors of the Ming and Qing dynasties fasted in preparation for rituals at the Altar of the God of Agriculture.

In 1755 (the 20th year of the Qianlong era of the Qing Dynasty), the palace's corridors and walls were renovated, forming the layout seen today, and it was renamed Qingcheng Palace. It became the place where emperors celebrated the successful completion of ceremonies honoring the God of Agriculture and their own ritual plowing of the Ceremonial Farmland.

Historical records note that civil and military officials would gather here to offer congratulations to the emperor upon the conclusion of the rites. The emperor would then bestow tea upon the officials. Following this, the Prefect of Shuntian and the county magistrates of Daxing and Wanping would report the number of completed furrows at the east side gate of Qingcheng Palace. Once the ceremony concluded, the emperor would depart by imperial carriage.

Exhibition Location: Qingcheng Palace at the Altar of the God of Agriculture

Exhibition Duration: Permanent

Organizer: Beijing Municipal Cultural Heritage Bureau

Official website: Altar of the God of Agriculture (Beijing Ancient Architecture Museum)

                  http://www.bjgjg.com

Sponsor: Beijing Central Axis Conservation Foundation

探

访

中

轴

CITY WALKS: BEIJING CENTRAL AXIS EXHIBITION SPECIAL

庆成宫原状陈设
Reconstructed Interior
Display of Qingcheng
Palace

庆成宫原状陈设
Reconstructed Interior Display of Qingcheng Palace

先农坛历史文化展

坐落于北京中轴线南端西侧的先农坛，是明清时期天子亲祭先农、亲耕耤田的皇家祭祀场所，于 1420 年建成，迄今已 600 余年。本展以较为全面的信息展示北京先农坛的历史及其蕴含的农耕祭祀文化内涵，分为"先农坛的变迁""亲耕亲祭大典""古代祭农文化"3 个部分，为观众展现了北京中轴线上这一宝贵文化遗产的历史变迁，展示了中国古代农耕文明重要承载地的历史风貌。

展览地点：北京先农坛神厨建筑群
展览时间：长期
主办单位：北京市文物局
官方网站：先农坛（北京古代建筑博物馆）
　　　　　http://www.bjgjg.com

Historical and Cultural Exhibition of the Altar of the God of Agriculture

Located on the west side of the southern end of Beijing Central Axis, the Altar of the God of Agriculture is an imperial sacrificial site where the emperor personally offered sacrifices to the God of Agriculture and personally farmed the Ceremonial Farmland during the Ming and Qing dynasties. It was completed in 1420 and has a history of over 600 years. This exhibition focuses on presenting comprehensive information about the history of the Altar and the cultural significance of farming and sacrificial rituals. It is divided into three parts: "Changes of the Altar of the God of Agriculture," "Grand Ceremony of Emperor Farming and Sacrificing," and "Ancient Agricultural Ritual Culture." It showcases the historical changes of this precious cultural heritage along Beijing Central Axis and presents the historical appearance of an important site that carried the ancient Chinese agricultural civilization.

Exhibition Location: The Divine Kitchen Complex at the Altar of the God of Agriculture

Exhibition Duration: Permanent

Organizer: Beijing Municipal Cultural Heritage Bureau

Official Website: Altar of the God of Agriculture (Beijing Ancient Architecture Museum)
　　　　　　　http://www.bjgg.com

先农坛历史文化展
Historical and Cultural Exhibition of the Altar of the
God of Agriculture

神仓历史文化展——神仓藏玉粒　五谷播天下

　　神仓建筑群是先农坛建筑群的重要组成部分，用于储存耤田收获的谷物。其中的神仓被誉为"天下第一仓"，为先农坛所独有，是将储藏的谷物转换为皇家祭祀礼仪祭品的重要场所。

　　"神仓历史文化展——神仓藏玉粒　五谷播天下"结合神仓建筑群的历史及建筑特点，以"神仓藏玉粒　五谷播天下"为主题，通过原状陈列和历史知识展示的形式，将神仓建筑群的原状、历史变迁过程，及其在中轴线祭祀礼仪中发挥的重要作用呈现给观众，也让与世隔绝了200多年的神仓建筑群第一次走进社会大众视野。

展览地点：北京先农坛神仓建筑群
展览时间：长期
主办单位：北京市文物局
官方网站：先农坛·北京古代建筑博物馆
　　　　　http://www.bjgg.com
资助单位：由北京文化中轴线保护公益基金会和联拓公司共同设立的"中海基金"资助

Divine Granary Complex Historical and Cultural Exhibition— Storing Grains and Spreading Crops

The Divine Granary Complex is an important part of the Altar of the God of Agriculture Complex, as it is used for storing grains harvested from the Ceremonial Farmland. The Divine Granary is renowned as the "NO.1 granary in China" and is unique to the Altar of the God of Agriculture. It serves as a significant place for transforming stored grains into royal sacrificial offerings during ceremonial rituals.

Combining the history and architectural features of the Divine Granary Complex and under the theme of "Storing Grains and Spreading Crops," the exhibition will showcases the original state and historical changes of the Divine Granary Complex, as well as its significant role in the sacrificial rituals along the central axis through the *in situ* display and historical knowledge introduction. The exhibition aims to present these aspects to the visitors to bring the Divine Granary Complex, which has been secluded from the public for over two hundred years, to the general public for the first time.

Exhibition Location: The Divine Granary Complex at the Altar of the God of Agriculture

Exhibition Duration: Permanent

Organizer: Beijing Municipal Cultural Heritage Bureau

Official Website: Altar of the God of Agriculture (Beijing Ancient Architecture Museum)
　　　　　http://www.bjgjg.com

Sponsor: Zhongteng Foundation, jointly established by the Beijing Central Axis Conservation Foundation
　　　　　and Tencent Holdings Limited

神仓历史文化展——
神仓藏玉粒　五谷播天下
Divine Granary Complex Historical and Cultural
Exhibition—Storing Grains and Spreading Crops

中国古代建筑展

中国古代建筑是中国古代劳动人民智慧的结晶，是世界建筑文化中的一颗明珠，是人类文明发展进步的重要见证。

本展览分为"中国古代建筑发展历程""中国古代建筑类型欣赏""中国古代建筑营造技艺""祭祀太岁——太岁坛复原陈列""匠人营国——中国古代城市"5个部分，通过较为丰富的展览形式和展品，为观众展现了内容丰富、形式多样的古代建筑文化。本展览深受大中小学生喜爱，已成为学生的第二课堂，对普及中国古代建筑文化知识有着不可替代的作用。本展览还从中国古代建筑文化这一角度讲述了北京中轴线的历史故事。

展览地点：北京先农坛太岁殿建筑群（太岁殿、拜殿、西配殿）

展览时间：长期

主办单位：北京市文物局

官方网址：先农坛（北京古代建筑博物馆）

http://www.bjgjg.com

Exhibition of Ancient Chinese Architecture

Ancient Chinese architecture is a unique gem in the world's architectural culture and serves as an important witness to the development and progress of human civilization. With its distinctive use of timber and earth materials, beam and arch structures, and vibrantly painted decorations, ancient Chinese architecture has formed its own system within the realm of world architectural culture. It is a crystallization of the wisdom of the ancient Chinese working people.

This exhibition is divided into five parts: "Development of Ancient Chinese Architecture," "Appreciation of Ancient Chinese Architectural Types," "Craftsmanship in Ancient Chinese Construction," "Sacrificing to the God of the Year—Display of the Reconstructed Altar of the God of the Year," and "Craftsmen and Ancient Chinese Cities." Through a diverse range of exhibition forms and artifacts, it showcases the rich cultural connotations and varied forms of ancient Chinese architecture. The exhibition has gained great popularity among students of different age groups and has become an important extracurricular activity for them, playing an irreplaceable role in promoting knowledge about ancient Chinese architecture. The exhibition also tells the historical stories of the Beijing Central Axis from the perspective of ancient Chinese architectural culture.

Exhibition Location: The Hall of the God of the Year Complex at the Altar of the God of Agriculture
(The Hall of the God of the Year, the Sacrificial Hall, and the West Side Hall)

Exhibition Duration: Permanent

Organizer: Beijing Municipal Cultural Heritage Bureau

Official Website: Altar of the God of Agriculture (Beijing Ancient Architecture Museum)
http://www.bjgjg.com

中国古代建筑展
Exhibition of Ancient Chinese Architecture

太岁殿东配殿及宰牲亭历史文化展

太岁殿东配殿展厅（南区）展览主题为"北京中轴线上的古建筑"。该展览以灯箱式展板与建筑模型相结合的展陈形式，通过解析北京中轴线上的古建筑结构特征与技艺特色，让公众领略北京中轴线上古建筑的文化内涵与魅力，让观众从古建筑这一侧面了解北京中轴线的历史文化。

宰牲亭展厅展览主题为"北京先农坛宰牲亭原状展示及馆藏古建筑模型展"。通过梳理宰牲亭的历史脉络，解读宰牲亭的祭祀功能、建筑特点，展示先农坛这一中轴线上古代皇家祭祀建筑群完整的历史风貌，并充分利用古建筑的空间，展示馆藏古建筑模型，让观众从多个角度了解中国古代建筑的结构特点和古人的聪明智慧。

展览地点：北京先农坛太岁殿东配殿及宰牲亭

展览时间：长期

主办单位：北京市文物局

官方网站：先农坛（北京古代建筑博物馆）

　　　　　http://www.bjgjg.com

赞助单位：由北京某企中轴线保护公益基金会和腾讯公司共同设立的"中轴基金"资助

Historical and Cultural Exhibition of the East Side Hall of the Hall of the God of the Year and the Pavilion for Preparing Animal Sacrifices

The exhibition hall of the East Side Hall of the Hall of the God of the Year (South Zone) has the theme of "Ancient Architecture on Beijing Central Axis." Through the combination of lightbox-style display panels and architectural models, the exhibition analyzes the structural features and craftsmanship characteristics of ancient architecture along Beijing Central Axis. It enables the public to appreciate the cultural connotations and charm of ancient architecture on Beijing Central Axis, allowing visitors to understand the historical and cultural significance of Beijing Central Axis through the perspective of ancient architecture.

The exhibition hall of the Pavilion for Preparing Animal Sacrifices has the theme of "In Situ Display of the Pavilion for Preparing Animal Sacrifices at the Altar of the God of Agriculture and Exhibition of Ancient Architectural Models in the Collection." By tracing the historical context of the Pavilion for Preparing Animal Sacrifices and interpreting its sacrificial functions and architectural features, the exhibition showcases the complete historical appearance of the ancient royal sacrificial architectural complex at the Altar of the God of Agriculture along the central axis. It also utilizes the space of ancient architecture to display a collection of ancient architectural models, allowing visitors to understand the structural features of ancient Chinese architecture and the wisdom of the ancient Chinese from various perspectives.

Exhibition Location: The East Side Hall of the Hall of the God of the Year and the Pavilion for Preparing Animal Sacrifices at the Altar of the God of Agriculture

Exhibition Duration: Permanent

Organizer: Beijing Municipal Cultural Heritage Bureau

Official Website: Altar of the God of Agriculture (Beijing Ancient Architecture Museum)
http://www.bjgjg.com

Sponsor: Zhongteng Foundation, jointly established by the Beijing Central Axis Conservation Foundation and Tencent Holdings Limited.

太岁殿东配殿及宰牲亭历史文化展

Historical and Cultural Exhibition of the East Side Hall of the Hall of the God of the Year and the Pavilion for Preparing Animal Sacrifices

永定门

邦国永定——永定门历史文化展

　　永定门为明清时期北京老城外城正南门，是北京外城 7 座城门中规制最高的一座，它承载着首都管理功能，也见证了不同时期的重要历史事件。"邦国永定——永定门历史文化展"介绍了永定门的历史脉络和建筑工艺，透过永定门的历史沧桑，揭示了"永定门"的和平内涵及当代意义。

展览地点：永定门城楼
主办单位：北京市东城区文物研究中心

Yongdingmen Gate

A National Guardian of Enduring Peace—Yongdingmen Gate Historical and Cultural Exhibition

Yongdingmen Gate is the southern gate of the central outer city of the old city of Beijing during the Ming and Qing dynasties. As the highest-level gate of the seven gates of the outer city, it carries the function of capital administration and witnesses important historical events throughout different periods. "A National Guardian of Enduring Peace—Yongdingmen Gate Historical and Cultural Exhibition" introduces the history and architectural craftsmanship of Yongdingmen Gate. Through the vicissitudes of Yongdingmen Gate's history, the exhibition reveals the peaceful connotation and contemporary significance of the Gate.

Exhibition Location: Yongdingmen Gate Tower

Organizer: Cultural Heritage Research Center of Dongcheng District, Beijing

邦国永定——永定门历史文化展
A National Guardian of Enduring Peace—Yongdingmen Gate Historical and Cultural Exhibition

永定门
Yongdingmen Gate

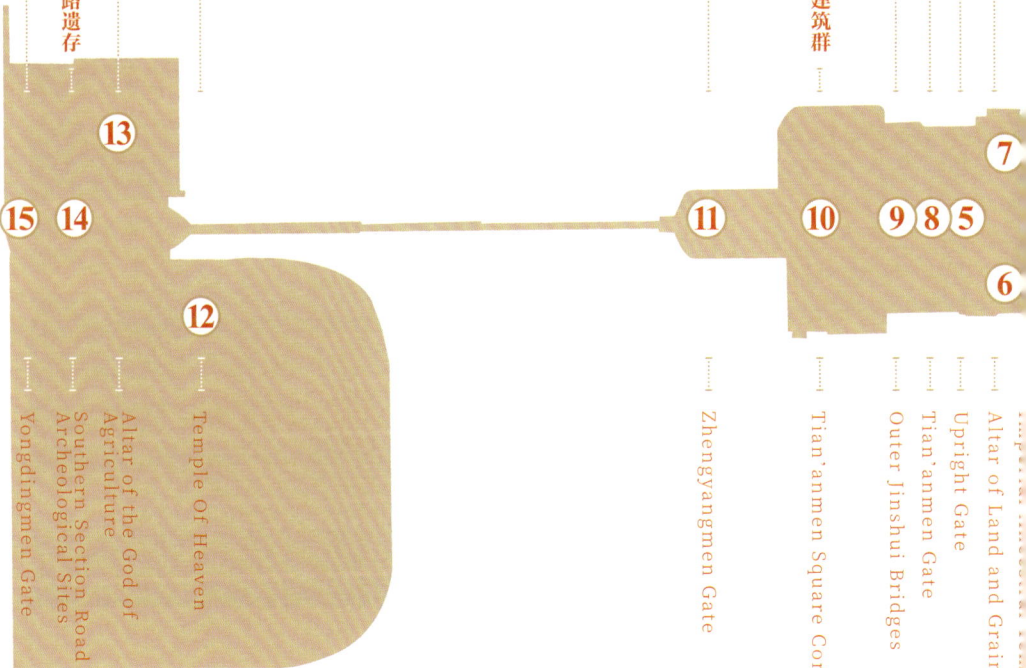

中轴线南段道路遗存
Southern Section Road Archeological Sites

先农坛
Altar of the God of Agriculture

天坛
Temple Of Heaven

正阳门
Zhengyangmen Gate

天安门广场及建筑群
Tian'anmen Square Complex

外金水桥
Outer Jinshui Bridges

天安门
Tian'anmen Gate

端门
Upright Gate

社稷坛
Altar of Land and Grain

⑬

⑮ ⑭

⑫

⑪

⑩ ⑨ ⑧ ⑤

⑦

⑥

钟鼓楼

万宁桥

景山

③ ② ①

Jingshan Hill

Wanning Bridge

Bell and Drum Towers

南 —— 北

　　北京中轴线作为重要的文化遗产，是古都北京的脊梁，承载着深厚的历史底蕴与中华民族的精神内涵。自形成以来，它串联起故宫、天坛、钟鼓楼等一系列历史建筑，以建筑语言书写着数百年间朝代的兴衰、社会的变革，见证了中华文明发展的关键进程，是当之无愧的人类文明瑰宝。

　　如今，随着时代的发展，北京中轴线被赋予新的价值与活力。"数字中轴"依托前沿数字化技术，通过三维建模、虚拟现实等手段，对中轴线进行全方位、高精度的数字化呈现，打破了时间与空间的局限，让全球受众得以跨越地域限制，沉浸式领略其风貌。公益中轴相关项目的推进同样成果斐然，众多志愿者、文化机构与社会力量积极参与，借助讲座、展览、研学等形式，广泛传播北京中轴线知识，增强了公众对文化遗产的保护意识。

As a significant heritage site, Beijing Central Axis forms the core framework of the ancient capital. It embodies profound historical depth and spiritual essence of the Chinese nation. Since its formation, the axis has connected a series of historic landmarks, including the Forbidden City, the Temple of Heaven, and the Bell and Drum Towers, using architectural language to narrate centuries of dynastic rise and fall and societal transformation. It has borne witness to and played a role in key moments of Chinese civilization, making it a true treasure of human civilization.

Today, with the passage of time, Beijing Central Axis has been imbued with new vitality and value. The "Digital Central Axis" initiative leverages cutting-edge technologies such as 3D modeling and virtual reality to provide a comprehensive and high-precision digital representation of the axis. This breaks the boundaries of time and space, enabling global audiences to experience its grandeur in an immersive manner, regardless of geographic constraints. Meanwhile, the Central Axis Benefits All initiative has also achieved remarkable progress. With active participation from volunteers, cultural institutions, and various sectors of society, the initiative promotes widespread awareness and appreciation of Beijing Central Axis through lectures, exhibitions, and educational programs, thereby enhancing public consciousness of cultural heritage conservation.

遗产中轴

《世界遗产名录》列入理由

标准iii：能为延续至今或业已消逝的文明或文化传统提供独特的或至少是特殊的见证。

北京中轴线为中华文明"中""和"文化传统提供了特殊的物质见证。北京中轴线不仅为延续至今的国家礼仪文化传统提供了独特见证，展现出 13 世纪至今都城规划对于礼仪和秩序的强调，展现出通过城市营造与治理寻求社会和谐安定的美好追求，而且为传统的城市管理方式提供了有力的物质见证。自肇建至今，它历经城市历史演进而持续地影响着城市发展，展现出传统规划理念持久的生命力。

标准iv：是一种建筑、建筑或技术整体、或景观的杰出范例，展现人类历史上一个（或几个）重要阶段。

北京中轴线以独具匠心的选址，整体展现了《考工记》所载传统都城理想范式的规划格局，富于层次、秩序而又蕴含对比、变化的建筑形式和城市景观，成为中国传统都城中轴线发展至成熟阶段的杰出范例，亦成为中国保存最为完好的传统都城中轴线建筑群。

Beijing Central Axis as a Heritage Site

Criterion (iii)：Bear a unique or at least exceptional testimony to a cultural tradition or to a civilization which is living or which has disappeared.

Beijing Central Axis provides an exceptional material testimony to the philosophy of "neutrality and harmony" prized in the Chinese tradition. It is a unique evidence to testify to the state ritual traditions that have been carried forward to this day, exhibiting the emphasis placed on rituals and order in capital city planning since the 13th century and embodying the pursuit of social harmony and stability through urban construction. It also stands as a vivid illustration of the traditional way of city management. Since its inception, Beijing Central Axis has continued to evolve and exert influence on the city's urban development, demonstrating the enduring vitality of planning tradition.

Criterion (iv)：Be an outstanding example of a type of building， architectural or technological ensemble or landscape which illustrates (a) significant stage(s) in human history.

Beijing Central Axis is an outstanding example representing the mature stage of the urban central axis of Chinese capitals, and also the best-preserved capital central axis in China, characterized by its unique siting, its urban layout demonstrating the paradigm of the ideal capital city as set out in the *Kaogongji* , and its hierarchical and well-ordered architectural form and urban landscape.

北京中轴线
Beijing Central Axis

北京中轴线
Beijing Central Axis

遗产新生

北京中轴线在申报世界遗产过程中，修缮了众多不同时期的历史遗存，起到了通过申报世界遗产来促进整个北京老城保护的作用。不可移动文物保护工程、古建筑修缮及仿古建筑建设工程[1]严格遵循文物保护的相关法规，维护北京中轴线的完整性和真实性，按照"原形制、原结构、原工艺、原材料"的原则，制定了相应的设计方案和保养维护措施。此外，随着北京中轴线界桩及标识牌建设项目[2]的落地实施，北京中轴线形成了统一的地界标志规范。界桩及标识牌设计充分考虑了北京中轴线作为线性遗产、历史城区类遗产的特点，对于北京中轴线文化遗产保护、价值传播具有重要意义，也为全国文化遗产标识体系建设应用提供了示范。

1. 从20世纪50年代起，首开房地集团负责实施了故宫、颐和园、恭王府、天坛、北海、雍和宫等千余项文物古建修缮和仿古建筑工程。

2. 北京中轴线界桩及标识牌建设项目由北京京企中轴线保护公益基金会和腾讯公司共同设立的"中腾基金"资助

Rebirth of Heritage

During the nomination process for World Heritage status, numerous historic sites and monuments from various periods along Beijing Central Axis were repaired, fulfilling the purpose of using the nomination as a means to promote the protection of the old city of Beijing. Projects involving the conservation of immovable cultural heritage, the repair of historic monuments, and the construction of traditional-style buildings[1] have all strictly followed relevant cultural heritage protection laws and regulations, ensuring the integrity and authenticity of Beijing Central Axis. In accordance with the principles of "original design, original structure, original craftsmanship, and original materials," corresponding design schemes and maintenance measures were developed.

In addition, with the implementation of the boundary marker and signage system for Beijing Central Axis[2], a standardized system of geographical markers has been established. The design of the boundary markers and signs fully reflects the characteristics of Beijing Central Axis as a linear heritage site and as part of a historic town. This initiative plays a significant role in the protection and value dissemination of the Beijing Central Axis cultural heritage and serves as a model for the application of signage systems in heritage sites across the country.

1. Since the 1950s, Shoukai Real Estate Development Group has undertaken over 100 projects for the repair of historic monuments and construction of traditional-style buildings, including those in the Forbidden City, the Summer Palace, Prince Gong's Mansion, the Temple of Heaven, Beihai Park, and the Lama Temple (Yonghegong).

2. The construction project for the boundary marker and signage system of Beijing Central Axis is funded by the Zhongteng Foundation, jointly established by the Beijing Central Axis Conservation Foundation and Tencent Holdings Limited.

遗产新生
Rebirth of Heritage

跨越时空[1]

北京中轴线继承了自周代开始的城市秩序和规划思想，是 3000 多年中国文化精神的载体。中轴线两侧的街巷胡同保持着特有的格局和肌理，使整个北京老城具有了强烈的整体感、稳定感和归属感。同时，北京中轴线也是不同社会阶层文化和生活的载体，外城普通百姓的生活，内城达官贵人的生活，皇城、宫城帝王的生活，全都在北京中轴线上反映出来。

北京中轴线体现了中华民族海纳百川的精神和中正平和的追求，也传达了中华文明中的一个重要理念，即人与自然和谐相处，人与人和谐相待，人的内心世界和谐安宁。

1. 中外合拍纪录片《跨越时空的北京中轴线》，通过展现北京中轴线 750 多年的传承演变过程，凸显北京中轴线作为活态文化遗产生生不息、历久弥新的特质，向国际观众展示了中华文化遗产的独特之处及其生命力。该纪录片由北京广播电视网络视听发展基金、国家文化产业发展专项资金、北京京企中轴线保护公益基金会和腾讯公司联合资助。

Spanning Time and Space[1]

Beijing Central Axis carries forward the principles for urban order and planning that date back to Zhou Dynasty, representing a continuous lineage of Chinese cultural spirit spanning 3,000 years. The alleys and hutongs along both sides of the axis retain their distinctive layout and texture, endowing the old city of Beijing with a strong sense of unity, stability, and belonging. At the same time, Beijing Central Axis serves as a vessel for the culture and everyday life of various social classes, from the lives of commoners in the Outer City, to the elites of the Inner City, and the emperors within the Imperial and Palace Cities, all of which are reflected along this historic line.

Beijing Central Axis also embodies the Chinese nation's spirit of inclusiveness and its pursuit of balance and harmony. It conveys a core tenet of Chinese civilization: the harmonious coexistence of humans and nature, mutual respect among people, and inner peace within the human spirit.

1. The China-foreign co-produced documentary *Crafting Civilization: Beijing Central Axis* traces over 750 years of the history and development of Beijing Central Axis, highlighting its enduring vitality as a living cultural heritage site. Through this narrative, the documentary showcases to international audiences the uniqueness and vitality of Chinese cultural heritage. The production is funded by the Beijing Radio and Television Network Audiovisual Development Fund, National Cultural Industry Development Special Fund, Beijing Central Axis Conservation Foundation, and Tencent Holdings Limited.

《跨越时空的北京中轴线》
Crafting Civilization Beijing Central Axis

漫步中轴

毛主席
纪念堂　　人民英雄
纪念碑　　天安门
广场　　天安门

　　前往雄伟挺拔的毛主席纪念堂，感受以毛泽东同志为核心的党的第一代革命领袖集体的人生风采和人格魅力；走近人民英雄纪念碑，了解在中国共产党领导下 28 年来反帝反封建的伟大革命斗争史实，感受中国特色的民族风格；来到庄严肃穆的天安门广场，观看升国旗仪式，在雄壮的歌声中体会祖国的强大和人民的团结；参观天安门城楼，加深对国家历史文化的理解，感受震撼人心的宏伟与庄严。

Scrolling the Central Axis

Searching for the "Backbone" on the Central Axis

Chairman Mao Memorial Hall	The Monument to the People's Heroes	Tian'anmen Square	The Tian'anmen Gate

Go to the majestic Chairman Mao Memorial Hall and experience the lifestyle and personal charm of the first generation of revolutionary leaders of the Communist Party of China (CPC) with Comrade Mao Zedong as the core; Approaching the Monument to the People's Heroes, learn about the historical facts of the great revolutionary struggle against imperialism and feudalism under the leadership of the CPC, and feel the national style with Chinese characteristics; Stand in the solemn and majestic Tian'anmen Square, witnessing the flag-raising, and appreciate the strength of the motherland and the unity of the people in the magnificent singing; Visit the Tian'anmen Gate Tower to deepen our understanding of the country's history and culture, and feel the awe inspiring grandeur and solemnity.

寻找中轴线上的"脊梁"
Searching for the "backbone" on the central axis

探访文化古都

永定门 〉 先农坛 〉 天坛 〉 正阳门及箭楼

　　来到永定门，了解其拆而复建的曲折经历，领略完整的北京中轴线格局；走进先农坛，在古代皇家祭祀建筑的庄严中，感受国泰民安、五谷丰登的喜悦；踏入天坛，在高大的祈年殿与神秘的回音壁中，体会天地之气的交融与深厚的历史沉淀；最后来到正阳门，观赏历经沧桑仍屹立于此的正阳门城楼与箭楼，了解古代军事防御思想和技术水平，感受古都北京的雄伟壮观。

Exploring the Ancient Cultural Capital

The Yongdingmen
Gate

The Altar of the
God of Agriculture

The Temple of
Heaven

The Zhengyangmen Gate
and Archery Towers

Begin at the Yongdingmen Gate, learning about its dismantling and reconstruction, and appreciate the full expanse of Beijing Central Axis. Step into the Altar of the God of Agriculture and, amid the solemnity of imperial sacrificial buildings, share in the joy of national peace and abundant harvests. Enter the Temple of Heaven, where the majestic Hall of Prayer for Good Harvests and the mysterious Echo Wall evoke the harmony between heaven and earth and the profound legacy of history. Conclude your journey at the Zhengyangmen Gate, admiring the enduring presence of the gate tower and archery tower that have withstood the test of time, and gain insight into ancient military defense concepts and technical achievements, an awe-inspiring encounter with the grandeur of Beijing as an ancient capital.

体验皇城底蕴

故宫博物院 〉 太庙 〉 社稷坛 〉 景山公园 〉 万宁桥 〉 鼓楼及钟楼

　　来到北京故宫博物院，参观中国明清两代 24 位皇帝的皇家宫殿，感受无与伦比的建筑杰作；踏入太庙，置身于明清两代皇室祖庙，感受皇家祭祀建筑群的庄严肃穆之气；前往社稷坛，参观明清两代帝王祭祀太社和太稷的神坛，领悟古人对国家、天下和黎民的理解；走进景山公园，驻足于元明清三代的皇家后苑中，领略整齐对称的布局神韵；移步皇城后门——地安门北面的万宁桥，感受消失了 700 余年的"水穿街巷"的历史景观；最后，来到鼓楼及钟楼，参观古老都城的报时中心，了解"天明击鼓催人起，入夜鸣钟催人息"的晨鼓暮钟制度。

Experiencing the Legacy of the Imperial City

The Palace Museum 〉 The Imperial Ancestral Temple 〉 The Altar of Land and Grain 〉 Jingshan Park 〉 Wanning Bridge 〉 The Drum and Bell Towers

Visit the Palace Museum in Beijing, where you can explore the imperial palace of 24 emperors from the Ming and Qing dynasties and experience an unparalleled architectural masterpiece. Step into the Imperial Ancestral Temple, the royal ancestral shrine of the Ming and Qing courts, and feel the solemn and dignified atmosphere of the imperial ritual building complex. Proceed to the Altar of Land and Grain, where emperors of the Ming and Qing dynasties worshipped the gods of land and grain, and reflect on the ancient understanding of nation, world, and people. Enter Jingshan Park, once the imperial garden of the Yuan, Ming, and Qing dynasties, and appreciate the harmony and elegance of its symmetrical layout. Move on to the Wanning Bridge, north of Di'anmen, the rear gate of the Imperial City, and sense the vanished landscape of "water flowing through the streets and alleys" that existed over 700 years. Finally, arrive at the Drum and Bell Towers, once the timekeeping center of the ancient capital, and learn about the traditional system of morning drums and evening bells, which awakened people at dawn and signaled rest at night.

体验皇城底蕴
Experiencing the legacy of the Imperial City

走进博物馆之城

国家自然博物馆 ⟩ 中国铁道博物馆正阳门馆 ⟩ 中国国家博物馆 ⟩ 故宫博物院 ⟩ 文化和旅游部恭王府博物馆 ⟩ 北京郭守敬纪念馆 ⟩ 北京市钟鼓楼文物保管所

　　探索国家自然博物馆，观赏大量珍贵的自然标本，深入了解生命的奥秘，感受自然界的奇妙与壮丽；踏入中国铁道博物馆正阳门馆，了解中国铁路百年历史发展与变迁；参观中国国家博物馆，置身于丰富的藏品中，感受中华 5000 多年文明的血脉绵延与灿烂辉煌；走进故宫博物院，尽享建筑美学的视觉盛宴；漫步至文化和旅游部恭王府博物馆，感受中国清代古建筑中的珍贵遗存，了解悠久的王府历史文化；进入北京郭守敬纪念馆，了解郭守敬一生的功绩及其对北京城市历史发展的贡献；来到北京市钟鼓楼文物保管所，探索报时中心的重要价值，在沉浸式的数字展览中，感受古老遗产焕发出的新生机；踏入全聚德博物馆，亲眼见证北京烤鸭这一国家级非遗的制作过程；最后，走进北京同仁堂博物馆，了解博大精深的传统中医药知识，体验中轴线上的京味文化和匠心传承。

Embracing the City of Museums

Natural History Museum of China ⟩ China Railway Museum (Zhengyangmen Branch) ⟩ National Museum of China ⟩ The Palace Museum ⟩ Prince Kung's Mansion Museum (under the Ministry of Culture and Tourism) ⟩ Beijing Guo Shoujing Memorial Hall ⟩ Beijing Bell and Drum Towers Cultural Relics Management Office

Explore the Natural History Museum of China, where a vast collection of precious natural specimens offers insight into the mysteries of life and the wonders and grandeur of the natural world. Step into the Zhengyangmen Branch of the China Railway Museum to trace over a century of development and transformation in China's railway history. Visit the National Museum of China, and amidst its rich collections, experience the enduring legacy and brilliance of over 5,000 years of Chinese civilization. Enter the Palace Museum and indulge in a visual feast of architectural aesthetics. Stroll to the Prince Kung's Mansion Museum, under the Ministry of Culture and Tourism, to admire a rare gem of Qing Dynasty architecture and explore the time-honored history and culture of royal mansions. At the Beijing Guo Shoujing Memorial Hall, gain a understanding of Guo Shoujing's lifelong achievements and his contributions to the historical development of Beijing as a city. Arrive at the Beijing Bell and Drum Towers Cultural Relics Management Office to explore the historical significance of Beijing's ancient timekeeping center, and experience the revitalization of this cultural heritage through immersive digital exhibitions. Finally, step into the Quanjude Museum to witness firsthand the making of Peking Duck, a national-level intangible cultural heritage element, and continue on to the Tongrentang Museum to learn about the profound knowledge of traditional Chinese medicine, immersing yourself in the flavors, craftsmanship, and cultural legacy that define Beijing Central Axis.

数字中轴

　　数字中轴[1]运用大数据、云计算、人工智能、区块链、知识图谱、新文创等新技术，深挖北京中轴线历史文化内涵，推动文化遗产数字化保护与传承，通过数字化保护、数字化活化和数字化传承，使数字化成为北京中轴线申遗的重要创新与关键标签。历经数十年修缮与恢复，并在全球首次以数字技术全过程参与世界遗产申报，北京中轴线正以崭新的面貌赓续传承。

1. 数字中轴是由北京市文物局、北京中轴线申遗保护工作办公室联合腾讯公司发起的项目。

Digital Central Axis

The World's First Full-process Participation in a World Cultural Heritage Nomination Using Digital Technology

The "Digital Central Axis"[1] initiative leverages emerging technologies such as big data, cloud computing, artificial intelligence, blockchain, knowledge graphs, and new digital cultural creativity to deeply explore the historical and cultural significance of Beijing Central Axis. It advances the digital preservation and transmission of cultural heritage through three key pillars: digital conservation, digital revitalization, and digital inheritance, making digital innovation a crucial hallmark of Beijing Central Axis's nomination for World Heritage status. Following decades of repair and revitalization, and as the world's first heritage site to undergo a full World Heritage nomination process powered entirely by digital technology, Beijing Central Axis is now being passed down with a renewed and vibrant look.

1. The "Digital Central Axis" initiative was jointly launched by the Beijing Municipal Cultural Heritage Bureau, the Beijing Central Axis Nomination and Conservation Office, and Tencent Holdings Limited.

北京中轴线数字资源库
Beijing Central Axis Digital Resources Library

"云上中轴"小程序
"Cloud Central Axis" Applet

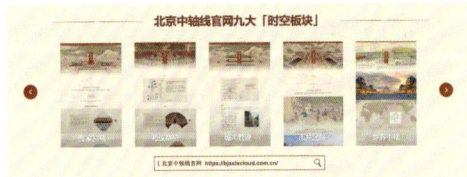

北京中轴线官方网站
Official website of Beijing Central Axis

让文化遗产在数字世界"永生"——数字化保护与数字化活化

全球首次运用游戏科技参与申遗的"数字中轴·时空舱""数字中轴·小宇宙"，基于"数字孪生+游戏科技"，应用游戏引擎及自研 PCG 技术、云游戏技术等，打造了全球首个超大型城市历史景观数字化沉浸式互动体验。从物理、历史和文化三个维度还原北京中轴线最美、最完整的一面，让更多人特别是年轻人参与到北京中轴线的保护工作中。

北京中轴线数字资源库创新构建北京中轴线"多模态"数字资源库，将北京中轴线数字资源开放授权，在多场景开展文创应用，探索"IP 版权+数字应用+公益反哺"模式。通过数字化技术处理，完整再现北京中轴线全貌，把存在于文档上、文物上的一些历史记忆符号用数字技术保存、处理、活化，让过去不可见、不可触的文物，特别是不可移动的文物都可视可感。

Bringing Cultural Heritage to Life in the Digital World — Digital Preservation and Digital Revitalization

The "Digital Central Axis · Time-Space Capsule" and "Digital Central Axis · Microcosm" represent the world's first use of gaming technology in a World Heritage nomination. Based on digital twin technology and powered by game engines, proprietary PCG (Procedural Content Generation) systems, and cloud gaming technology, together they create the world's first super large-scale immersive digital interactive experience of an urban historical landscape. From the physical, historical, and cultural dimensions, the project restores the most beautiful and complete representation of Beijing Central Axis, engaging a wider audience in its protection and promotion, especially younger generations.

The Beijing Central Axis Digital Resources Library, as a pioneering "multimodal" digital archive, enables open access to Central Axis digital assets, promoting their integration into diverse cultural and creative contexts. It also explores a model of "intellectual property rights + digital applications + public-interest feedback." Through digital technologies, the full panorama of Beijing Central Axis is reconstructed, preserving, processing, and revitalizing historical memory encoded in documents and artifacts. It allows previously unseen or inaccessible cultural relics, especially immovable heritage, to become visible, and tangible.

让文化遗产走进生活——数字化传承

科技的力量正帮助社会公众通过线上、线下相结合的方式，参与记录并保护身边的文化遗产。数字中轴项目产品化构建"数字打更人"志愿者体系，并沉淀文化遗产"场景码"通用工具。通过招募北京中轴线数字"打更人"，让更多人能够通过数字技术深度了解北京中轴线的信息，随时监测其保护状况并提出意见。

Bringing Cultural Heritage into Everyday Life — Digital Transmission

The power of technology is enabling the public to participate in documenting and protecting cultural heritage through a combination of online and offline approaches. The Digital Central Axis project has developed a product-based "Digital Watchkeeper" volunteer system and introduced a universal tool for cultural heritage — "Scene Code" tagging. By recruiting Beijing Central Axis Digital "Watchkeepers", more people are now able to engage with in-depth digital content about Beijing Central Axis, monitor its preservation status in real time, and contribute their own insights, empowering broader public participation in cultural heritage protection through digital means.

数字中轴·小宇宙
Digital Central Axis · Microcosm

北京中轴线数字"打更人"
Beijing Central Axis Digital "Watchkeepers"

数字中轴·时空舱
Digital Central Axis · Time-Space Capsule

公益中轴

北京京企中轴线保护公益基金会于 2019 年成立，是目前北京市唯一一家专职于北京中轴线遗产保护与传承的公益慈善机构，致力于推动北京中轴线公益事业发展。厚重的文化遗产，正在以更灵巧、更时尚的表达方式呈现在世人面前。自 2021 年起，北京中轴线文化遗产传承与创新大赛[1] 开始举办。一大批优秀人才和优质项目在比赛中脱颖而出，为北京中轴线的保护传承注入新的活力。在"印记北京中轴线——大众篆刻作品展"[2]中，不同形式的作品以小见大，使观众切身感受到中国传统城市建设中所追求的天地和谐的文化理念，进一步增强了全社会共同保护好历史文化遗产的意识与担当。大型油画《壮美中轴》则全景式呈现了北京中轴线的独特魅力，巨型脱胎漆画《永恒中轴》展示着以古映今的期待和以今待古的创新与包容，两幅作品现均展藏于正阳门城楼内。[3]

1. 北京中轴线文化遗产传承与创新大赛由北京市文物局、北京中轴线申遗保护工作办公室、北京中轴线遗产保护中心（北京世界文化遗产监测中心）主办

2. 2024 年 7 月至 10 月，由北京京企中轴线保护公益基金会联合中华世纪坛艺术馆等多家机构举办

3. 《壮美中轴》由著名画家刘宇一创作，由北京京企中轴线保护公益基金会与复兴之路文化艺术发展有限公司共同策划并资助，由中国榫楔博物馆捐赠画框及底座的设计与制作。《永恒中轴》由沈绍安漆艺博物馆创作，由正信慈善基金会捐赠于北京京企中轴线保护公益基金会

Beijing Central Axis for Public Interest

The Beijing Central Axis Conservation Foundation, established in 2019, is the only public charitable organization in Beijing dedicated exclusively to the conservation and inheritance of Beijing Central Axis. The foundation is committed to advancing public initiatives related to Beijing Central Axis.

Profound cultural heritage is now being presented to the world through more dynamic and fasionable forms of expression. Since 2021, the Beijing Central Axis Cultural Heritage Inheritance and Innovation Competition[1] has been held annually. A large number of outstanding talents and high-quality projects have emerged from the competition, injecting new vitality into the preservation and transmission of Beijing Central Axis. In the "Impressions of Beijing Central Axis — Public Seal Carving Exhibition,"[2] works in diverse forms embody grand ideas through small details, allowing visitors to personally experience the traditional Chinese urban ideal of harmony between heaven and earth. The exhibition further enhances public awareness and a sense of responsibility for the protection of historical and cultural heritage. The monumental lacquer painting *Eternal Central Axis* conveys a vision of interpreting the past through the present and embracing the ancient with innovation and inclusivity. The large-scale oil painting *Magnificent Central Axis* presents a panoramic view of the unique charm of Beijing Central Axis. Both works are now on display and housed within the Zhengyangmen Gate Tower.[3]

1. The Beijing Central Axis Cultural Heritage Inheritance and Innovation Competition is organized by the Beijing Municipal Cultural Heritage Bureau, the Beijing Central Axis Nomination and Conservation Office, and the Beijing Central Axis Heritage Conservation Center (Beijing World Cultural Heritage Monitoring Center).

2. From July to October 2024, the event was organized by the Beijing Central Axis Conservation Foundation in partnership with various institutions including the China Millennium Monument (Beijing World Art Museum).

3. *Magnificent Central Axis* was created by renowned artist Liu Yuyi and jointly curated and sponsored by the Beijing Central Axis Conservation Foundation and Fuxingzhilu Culture and Art Development Co., Ltd. The frame and base were designed and produced with the support of the China Red Sandalwood Museum. *Eternal Central Axis* was created by Shen Shao'an Lacquer Art Museum and donated by the Zhengjia Charity Foundation to the Beijing Central Axis Conservation Foundation.

《永恒中轴》脱胎漆
The monumental lacquer pain
Eternal Central Axis

北京中轴线文化遗产传承与创新大赛及 "印记北京中轴线——大众篆刻作品展" 作品
Works from the Beijing Central Axis Cultural Heritage Inheritance and Innovation Competition and
the "Impressions of Beijing Central Axis — Public Seal Carving Exhibition"